D1084502

MEASUREMENT OF RESPONSIBILITY

MEASUREMENT OF RESPONSIBILITY

A Study of Work, Payment, and Individual Capacity

ELLIOTT JAQUES

A HALSTED PRESS BOOK

JOHN WILEY & SONS
New York

Published in the U.S.A.
by Halsted Press, a Division
of John Wiley & Sons Inc.,
New York

Library of Congress Cataloging in Publication Data

Jaques, Elliott.
Measurement of Responsibility.

"A Halsted Press book."
Includes bibliographical references.
1. Wages. 2. Job evaluation. 3. Responsibility.
I. Title.
HD4915.J3 1972 331.2'2 72-5856
ISBN 0-470-44020-1

Printed in Great Britain by
Biddles Ltd, Guildford, Surrey, England

PREFACE

ALTHOUGH this book was first published fifteen years ago, it still gives the best account of how the time-span method of measuring responsibility in work was first developed. Both the description of the research and the theoretical considerations still stand. Any changes which have taken place are in the refinement in method of time-span measurement. These refinements are described in *Time-Span Handbook.**

The description in the Introduction of how this book was published will explain why it is a difficult task to acknowledge the assistance I have received with its preparation. Many hundreds of individuals in the firm have been directly involved in the work that has led up to it. Each of the discussions we have had and the reports they have worked through have their repercussions in these pages. I should like to mention those who were members of the firm's Works Council during the course of the work described, as the means of acknowledging the contribution of the individual members they represented, as well as the work they contributed in their roles as representatives.

The members of the Works Council were:

Mr. W. B. D. Brown—Managing Director. *Grade I Staff Members:* Mr. P. G. Forrester, Mr. R. Joy, Mr. P. D. Liddiard. *Grade II Staff Members:* Mr. A. E. Burke, Mr. J. Horne, Mr. C. Le Blond, Mr. A. G. Oram, Mr. R. Salter,

* Elliott Jaques, *Time-Span Handbook*, Heinemann, London, 1964.

Mr. K. Seymour, Mr. F. Shaw, Mr. H. G. Wisher. *Grade III Staff Members:* Mr. W. H. Crittenden, Mr. M. J. Coviello, Mr. F. I. Flack, Mr. R. W. Knott, Mr. A. J. Kroneck, Mr. E. C. Lucking, Mr. D. E. Nichols, Mr. J. W. Valentine, Mr. A. M. Wardrop. *Works Committee Members:* Mr. A. E. Bond, Mr. A. G. Cannon, Mr. L. A. Carran, Mr. T. C. Challinger, Mr. F. Cooper, Mr. J. Dalziel, Miss R. Healey, Mr. S. J. Healy, Mr. G. C. Hefford, Mr. T. Hungerford, Mr. W. H. Morton, Mr. G. Nicholas, Mr. J. A. Radley, Mr. F. G. Woods.

The officers of the Works Council during this period were: Dr. G. H. Gange—Chairman; Miss R. Fowler and Mr. J. West—Secretaries.

Of the above members of the Works Council, the following were in addition members of the Steering Committee of the Council, which was responsible for the work of the social-analyst:

Dr. G. H. Gange—Chairman; Miss R. Fowler, Mr. J. West—Secretaries; Mr. P. G. Forrester, Mr. W. H. Morton—Vice-Chairmen; and Mr. T. C. Challinger, Mr. P. G. Forrester, Mr. E. C. Lucking, Mr. W. H. Morton, Mr. G. Nicholas, Mr. A. G. Oram, Mr. A. M. Wardrop, Mr. F. G. Woods.

In addition, I must refer to the special help I have had from certain members who have worked on the manuscript. Mr. D. J. Clarkson, Mr. E. C. Lucking, Mr. W. H. Morton, Mr. G. Nicholas, have read and carefully criticized parts of it, and I have incorporated many of their suggestions. To Mr. W. B. D. Brown and Mr. J. M. M. Hill I must add further thanks for the painstaking manner in which they have gone through the whole of the manuscript in draft form. Their comments have been the source of some major revisions as well as many minor ones.

Miss Rhoda Fowler, who typed the manuscript, has done much more than secretarial work. She has been involved in many of the events described in her capacity as secretary to the Works Council, and its Steering Committee. Her knowledge and experience thus gained, and her genuine and cooperative interest, have been of the greatest help in preparatory work, and in assuring the accuracy of the description.

CONTENTS

individuals or groups not present, and not making recommendations or arbitrating in favour of one group or another. In order to carry out these principles, he has limited his relationships with members of the factory to strictly formal contacts that have to do with project work sanctioned by the Works Council. He has no personal relationships with Glacier members.

It was thought that by thus maintaining the social analyst's independent role in the factory, assistance could be given most effectively to those groups or individuals who sought help with a problem. If this assumption proved correct, it was anticipated that help would be sought on increasingly difficult problems, and so lead to deeper analysis of areas of the life of the factory that usually remain inaccessible except to those immediately involved. In this way it was hoped to overcome one of the difficult barriers in social research—to gain contact with problems of importance that in ordinary circumstances might remain outside the orbit of deeper analysis and resolution. The present work on status and grading problems has been made possible by this relationship.

A publication policy was instituted that is consistent with the independent social-analytic role. This policy—sought for technical reasons, and not imposed by the firm—requires that nothing is published outside the Company that has not been made public inside the Company at its Works Council meetings. The work being currently reported in this book has been published under these conditions. It comprises material that was worked through first of all with individuals. This material—with the authorization of the individuals—was then combined and built up into more general reports, which were then submitted either to representative or executive groups of which the individuals were members, and then, by the same process of build-up, to the Works Council.

INTRODUCTION

I

THE industrial scene continues to be disturbed by recurring difficulties in settling wage disputes in the absence of a defined wage and salary structure. The methods to be described herein might be considered to suggest a possible route towards a systematic pattern of financial reward in relation to the level of work done. These methods have been developed in the course of social consultancy work carried out in conjunction with a London engineering factory.

This consulting work has followed on from an applied social research project carried out in the same factory[1] between 1948 and 1951—financed by a Government research grant. The purpose of this research had been to explore in depth various aspects of industrial life within a single industrial unit. During this research phase, a number of changes had occurred in the Company, changes to which the research had contributed in such work as: an analysis and work-through of the problem of changing from piece-rates to flat rates in one department; an analysis of the work

[1] The Company is the Glacier Metal Company, and the work in the research phase—carried out in collaboration between the Company and a research team from the Tavistock Institute of Human Relations—has been reported in Elliott Jaques, *The Changing Culture of a Factory* (London: Tavistock Publications, 1951), and in articles in the journal *Human Relations*, contributed by A. K. Rice, J. M. M. Hill, E. L. Trist, and Elliott Jaques.

and functions and responsibilities of the Company's Works Council and representative organization; analyses, carried out at their request, on problems experienced by such diverse groups as the Works Committee, an executive group known as the Superintendents' Committee, and the top management group.

At the end of this period, when the Government research grant finance came to an end, the Company decided to carry on for itself the kind of work that had been done. It was the unanimous conclusion of its Works Council[1] that the work that had been done up till that time had been of practical benefit to the Company. They were in favour of continuing on a limited scale to see what further results might be achieved. The plan ultimately adopted was that the author should act on a part-time basis as a consulting social-analyst, responsible to the Works Council. This relationship, which is considered in detail in the next section, continues at the present time.

With the start of the new relationship in January 1952, there was a continuation of work on the above lines. Among the projects undertaken were, for example, an extensive analysis of the Company's total executive organization; the continuation of work with representative bodies; and work with a planning group charged with the responsibility to design and develop a management-training programme. There had been a striking absence of contact, however, with a range of problems—openly recognized in the firm—having

---

[1] The Company's Works Council is a body comprising fourteen members: the Managing Director plus thirteen elected members representative of the hourly-rated operators and the various grades of staff. Its Chairman is an independently elected member. The Company's policy requires that the Works Council shall consider any matters whatever. Agreement on the Council must be by unanimous decision, and no changes in the policy considered by the Council are made without this unanimous agreement. In the absence of such agreement, the previous policies or established precedents are continued. Cf. Chapter V, *The Changing Culture of a Factory* for a description of the development of the Council's policy-making responsibility and its mode of operation.

to do with status and grading, and with staff salaries and hourly-rated wages. Then, in September 1952, the work done with the Company radically changed in this respect. This change came about as a result of a request from an elected committee representing a section of the staff, to help it with an analysis of its own views about staff status and grading. The project, which thus started as a limited analysis of salary structure, status, and grading as it affected one section of the staff, eventually grew into an analysis of salary and wage differentials, status and grading, and promotion, selection, and appointments procedures, as these affected the Company as a whole. In order to appreciate how this development occurred, and to assess the findings from it, it will be necessary to understand the particular nature of the working relationship between the social-analyst and the members of the Company.

II

The relationship between the consultant and the firm was defined, after many months of discussion, in a document finally adopted by the Works Council in October 1952. This document laid down that he should be responsible to the Works Council through its Steering Committee—the Steering Committee being the executive committee of the Council, acting on its behalf between meetings. His responsibilities were defined as providing such professional services as might assist the working of the Company's organization. These professional services included: research on behalf of the Steering Committee; technical assistance on problems of social organization and group relations to members in their executive roles or as representatives, or to executive or representative groups or committees; assistance in a work-through role to groups who wished either to examine their own relationships in a general way, or to tackle difficulties in relationships that might be standing in the way of efficient work or progress.

A matter of considerable interest and importance was to discover means whereby the professional independence of the social-analyst could be assured. His contract was established on an annual basis, running from January to December. It was to be reviewed in June each year, so that if it was decided to terminate the contract there would be a six-month period during which any active work could be completed. Because wage and salary levels were not matters of public discussion in the firm (a matter that eventually became of some importance in the work to be reported), a special mechanism was devised for settling fees. The fee paid was to be set by the Managing Director, within terms of reference agreed in the Council as to the comparable executive level at which payment should be fixed. The point of this contract was to define the social-analyst's position not as a member of the Company but as somebody outside the Company who was available to assist any of its members. The contract has been reviewed and continued on this basis each year since that time. The review is by the Company's Works Council, it being a condition of the contract that the members of this body should be unanimously in accord for the contract to continue for another year.

The independence of role has been further defined by the conditions established for the social-analyst's work within the factory. Any section of the Company, or any member, or group of members, may apply directly to him for his services. Work can proceed so long as it has the endorsement of those immediately concerned, either directly or through their representatives acting on their behalf. Complete confidentiality is maintained. The members of the group concerned can talk about whatever they wish; the social-analyst for his part confining himself to analysing what is said—commenting on relationships within the immediate group, and on their discussion, to aid understanding and working-through of the difficulties—but most definitely not discussing any

PART I

The Problem

CHAPTER I

The Recurrence of Payment Disputes

I

THE problem with which we are here concerned is how to determine the appropriate payment and status for individuals for the work they do. By appropriate is meant a payment and status accorded in such a manner that each one has a sense of fair and just return for his work. It also means a pattern of payment that is economically sound.

Our problem is a complex one. It is framed by the wider question of how the general wage and salary structure of industry is arrived at. It requires a definition of work. It includes the problem of how to assess the ability of people so as to ensure that they have jobs appropriate to that ability. And it calls for principles that can provide for stability in the arrangements made, while at the same time making due allowance for the changes that occur in people and the changes occuring in the work that has to be done.

The present book is an interim report, deriving from work on the above problem carried out in just one industrial organization.[1] In the course of this work, some methods have been developed and ideas elaborated that suggest lines along which these problems may be more objectively appraised.

---

[1] A detailed description of the Company can be found in Elliott Jaques, *The Changing Culture of a Factory* (London: Tavistock Publications, 1951).

These developments comprise: a means to explore and to analyse manual and non-manual work objectively; a method that may give an objective measure of the level of work or responsibility; and some propositions about the possible existence of explicit and definable salary and wage differentials emerging from the use of the methods to be described. The conclusions to be drawn will be limited to industry.

II

The problem of status and payment is made more complex because it evokes powerful emotions—emotions about economic security and about the value attributed to one's own work as compared with that of others. The big issue of differentials is at stake—differentials in payment and in status, differentials between individuals and between groups. What commonly occurs is that a person or a body of people complains of losing ground relative to some other persons or bodies. They may feel this because they consider they are getting left behind by other persons or groups who are bettering their position. They may consider that somebody below them is catching up. Or they may consider that they have simply been underpaid or under-recognized for too long. Solutions to these problems are notoriously unstable. An adjustment that satisfies one body leads to the same problem arising for others, who then consider that their position has worsened. The consequent situation, with its indecisiveness and fluidity, is ordinarily held to be intractable as far as objective analysis is concerned. It is treated as though it is resolvable, in the final analysis, only within the framework of group pressures. The strongest forces are supposed to get the best of the matter.

One of the underlying difficulties in these arguments—and, it is suggested, a very important difficulty—is that, although there is a scale in terms of money for expressing amount of payment, there is no equivalent measure for individual capacity or for level of work.[1] In the absence of a measuring yardstick, argument and negotiation take place on the basis of assumptions and opinions about capacity and level of work. Thus, for example, if it is argued that one body of people has been losing ground to another with respect to payment, it is usually assumed that the level of work carried out by the two bodies has remained unchanged. It is also frequently assumed that the bodies continue to be made up of the same kinds of person as previously. These assumptions are at the core of the matter. Only to the extent that they are true does the argument hold that the gap between two bodies is narrowing or widening. But such assumptions leave a great deal of room for difference of opinion. Without some yardstick of comparison, the differences remain matters of emotional debate—and make for perverseness and rigidity in dispute. Even though the participants—labour and management alike—may earnestly try to find a way out of the deadlock, they nevertheless find themselves unable to do so. One of the consequences is the paralysing kind of industrial stress that may flare up over differentials.

It is of special importance to have a yardstick for measuring level of work, because of the widespread endorsement of the principle that payment should be directly related to the level of work done. This principle is commonly stated in the slogan 'the rate for the job'. But the large question that remains is how to measure the job. Everyone knows that it is possible, in a rough and ready way, to compare jobs—to recognize that this one is a more important or a bigger job than that one, or that this category of job is growing in skill and responsibility, or that those jobs have diminished in size

[1] It should be noted that *level* of work as here used must be distinguished from *quantity* of work. By level of work is meant what is usually referred to as size, or amount or intensity of responsibility in a job, or its importance. Quantity of work, on the other hand, refers to the amount of work to be done, irrespective of the level of responsibility involved. Thus we may speak of a certain quantity of work of a given level.

and are no longer as big as they were. But intuitive judgment of this type does not prove very helpful in a wage-negotiation situation when people's levels of income are dependent upon the results. Intuitive judgments are too coarse for such a purpose. And they are not only too coarse. The making of intuitive comparisons between jobs as a means of settling rates of pay suffers from other very great defects as well: people do not look at jobs in the same way; nor are they equally familiar with different jobs; nor, since jobs change, do they necessarily know a job today because they have done so at some time in the past; nor are they necessarily even talking about the same job, since the same job title can often cover a multitude of different kinds of work.

Despite the difficulties cited, making intuitive judgments about work is in common use as a means of assessing and agreeing the payment and status for given jobs in particular establishments. Much of job evaluation is based on such judgment—although the largely intuitive basis is often obscured behind the apparent, but simulated, objectivity to be obtained by using rating scales that give varying numbers of points to various aspects of a job. Judgment of this intuitive kind, while possibly having a limited use under local conditions, is of no use at all in negotiations affecting numbers of people in widely distributed establishments. Such negotiations require statements about work and about jobs in terms of principle. Principle requires explicit statement in words. Intuitive judgment is difficult, if not impossible, to frame in words. So long as judgment about work remains intuitive, negotiation in terms of principle remains impossible.

III

The yardsticks that are currently used in assessing and describing work whose payment is in question may be divided into two main categories: work yardsticks and personal yardsticks. The work yardsticks relate to comparisons between jobs on the basis of various aspects of responsibility that they have in common. The personal yardsticks relate to comparisons between jobs on the basis of comparisons between the persons who would be required to do the job in a reasonable and efficient way.

The first category of yardsticks—the work yardsticks—includes such factors as: physical weight of the work, distance travelled, danger, accuracy required, speed of work required, cleanliness, discomfort or dirtiness, quality of finish, numbers of subordinates controlled, seriousness of the effect of negligence, complexity or straightforwardness, and value of the materials worked with. Of such characteristics, serious scrutiny will show that all but three—danger, discomfort, and dirtiness—are likely to be misleading if taken by themselves, or together, as yardsticks for measuring and comparing jobs. And these three are factors relevant to the granting of special additional payments over and above a prescribed rate for a job, rather than a basis for a rate structure itself.

Accuracy required in work often arouses great passion in discussion. Working to fine tolerances, for example, is considered by those doing it as an argument for higher rates than for doing rough-finish work. What is often left out of account in such argument is the quality and character of the tooling—there being little virtue in operating a machine tool that does fine work that is checked with an automatic gauge, as compared with work that relies upon the sensibility of the operator or craftsman himself. And the same considerations would apply to quality of finish. Speed of work, like the foregoing factors, may make a job more difficult, or may not affect it at all. A job that includes as one of its aspects copy-typing at fifty words per minute need not be any more difficult as a job than one requiring forty words per minute, although it may be more difficult to keep going at the higher rate for any length of time.

Numbers of subordinates controlled is a favourite index of

size of job. It is probably true in many cases that if the number of subordinates under one's control in the same job increases, then one's responsibility is increasing. But it need not be true. An increase in the number of subordinates granted for carrying out an increasing number of laid-down administrative duties could reflect a decrease in responsibility. And a junior foreman with a number of subordinates is not necessarily doing a bigger job than, for example, a designer working on his own on a new machine-tool but having no subordinates at all.

The complexity or apparent straightforwardness of a job are other favourite indices of its importance or degree of responsibility. To say that a particular job is complex is to praise it; and to call it routine, a term of disparagement. The difficulty is to signify what is meant. Whether a task is complex or routine is often a matter on which competent judges may well disagree. And to the person unfamiliar with a job's requirements, what seems merely routine may be a much more complex task concealed under apparent ease of performance. So also such factors as the value of the articles or equipment worked with, the weight of work handled, the distances travelled, may have everything or nothing to do with size of responsibility. They are not sufficient in themselves as criteria for measurement—as yardsticks—and their use for such a purpose may often become quite incongruous.

The second category of yardsticks—the personal yardsticks (those based on the idea that jobs can be compared by comparing the persons needed to do them)—proves no more helpful. Examples of such yardsticks are: the skill, training and qualifications, experience or length of service, required in order to do a job; or other personality characteristics such as courage, resourcefulness, determination, reliability, and imagination. Such criteria, it is true, are quite general, in that to some degree, however slight, they apply to most jobs. But once again experience shows that they are extremely difficult to apply in practice in comparing jobs. This difficulty is well known, for instance, in the job evaluation methods that make use of rating scales for assessing the relative importance of jobs by rating the amounts of such qualities required in them.

In the first place, all these personal qualities are notoriously difficult to measure. Even the criterion of training, which seems simpler than some of the others, presents difficulties in comparing, for example, a five-year apprentice course, a four-year University course, and a ten-year period of on-the-job experience: and managing directors' jobs, in particular, are difficult to express in terms of the amount or type of training required. As for the other psychological criteria, their assessment leads into all kinds of subjective comparisons, admirably suited for ensnaring negotiators in emotional and partisan argument—with which society has become quite familiar in reading about the wage-differential disputes that afflict it. These arguments are hardly calculated to help in getting a satisfactory and lasting solution to the problems with which the criteria are supposed to deal.

IV

It is questionable whether either of these categories contains a single yardstick, or combination of yardsticks, that makes possible anything other than an apparent or illusory objectivity in discussion, in comparing jobs of work, and in negotiating the payment to be made for them. But perhaps one of the most serious difficulties in using such criteria is that sometimes, in very limited circumstances and for limited periods of time, they work. It may happen, for example, that for a given group, say, of machining operations, the smallness of the tolerances required may conform to what is felt to be the size of the job and to its value as far as payment is concerned. Agreement reached on such a basis, it is suggested, may be quite misleading, and a potential source of trouble. For the character of work, in ordinary circumstances, does not remain unchanged. Slight or gross modifications to one or other of the machines are introduced. As the market changes, customers' demands change, the product changes, and the individual operations change. The direction such changes will take is often difficult to foresee. The rate at which the changes are likely to occur is even more difficult to foresee. But one thing is a matter of common experience, and that is that, as the changes occur, the old criteria for comparing jobs tend no longer to work, and new aspects emerge as being of greater consequence under the changed methods of work. Then the cycle of discovering the most relevant criteria and of developing a satisfactory structure of payment begins again.

The problems outlined will be familiar to those with experience of industry. Another, and perhaps more far-reaching, difficulty will also be familiar. Not one of the criteria of the type outlined above can be used for comparing jobs of different types. This is true whether the criteria are taken singly, or together, with or without allowances or ratings for relative importance. Postmen cannot be compared with milkmen, porters with railway engineers, invoice clerks with draughtsmen, machine operators with typists, electricians with research technicians. The criteria simply do not apply in the same way to different jobs. Some, such as distance travelled, apply to some jobs, and not to others. Others, such as number of subordinates, or accuracy of work, may apply to all, but simply do not have the same relevance or meaning in one set of jobs as they would have in another.

With respect to the personal yardsticks, even if the psychological factors on which they are based could be measured, they would still beg the question of the rate for the job, substituting for it the rate for the person or grade of person. There is a widespread desire in industry to keep free from the use of such criteria. They lead to invidious comparisons being made between people, or between groups or categories of people. Such comparisons can be argued but not resolved so far as value in terms of relative income levels is concerned. And yet, despite the desire to keep away from such comparisons, industrial negotiations about rates frequently take place, without its being recognized, in terms not of the rate for the job but of the rate for the person in the job. Thus, for example, talking about rates for skilled, semi-skilled, and unskilled work is talking in terms of a psychological description of work—although it is not commonly recognized as such. It describes a job as requiring a 'skilled', or 'semi-skilled', or 'unskilled' person to do it. And while seemingly useful for describing categories of work on a very broad basis for an industry as a whole, there is a great deal of everyday experience to show that using such criteria brings about disruptive consequences on the shop floor. These consequences are to put a worker in the unenviable, difficult, and often irritating or frustrating position of having to argue that he has become as skilled as the next man, and that his job has become as skilled as well. His manager, replying in kind, then involves them in a discussion, equally disagreeable to both, of his opinion of that worker compared with his opinion of others. Whatever the outcome, a certain amount of feeling has been stirred, which, with the best will on both sides, may not readily be forgotten because of the particular framework of the discussion. Although we have used the illustration of a worker and his manager, it may be recognized that such argument may occur at any level in industry.

V

Negotiations about payment using seemingly objective criteria such as those outlined above may readily and easily revert, in a completely unrecognized way, to mere argument over differences in opinion based upon differences in intuitive judgment about jobs. Such argument, heightened and fanned by the wishes and desires aroused in the contending parties, is not only not held within the helpful grip of an agreed and objective frame of reference. It may be further exaggerated and distorted precisely because it is carried on within a framework that is presumed to be objective, but is really not, and so adds the worry and complication of vagueness and uncertainty, without its being quite apparent from just what quarter the obscurity is emanating.

It may be asked whether the circumstances described do not constitute a factor of some importance in the difficulties experienced over the negotiation of differentials in contemporary industrial life—difficulties strongly experienced not only between unions and employers, workers and staff, but also between various grades of worker, and various grades of staff, and between trade unions themselves. The lack of an objective foundation upon which to pin discussion about differentials may not commonly be held to be a primary cause of industrial discord. But it cannot be denied that it does contribute to suspicion and discord in negotiation; and it certainly does not facilitate agreement. An understanding of the consequences arising out of the framework currently in use may help to make understandable the very great difficulties experienced even by those with a genuine and hard-headed desire to resolve wage and salary questions in a fair and realistic way, but who nevertheless find themselves locked in painful and unwanted negotiation whose outcome may at the very best be a compromise. Such compromises, because they do not resolve any fundamental issues, lead only to the hope that they will last as long as possible.

The foregoing difficulties were encountered in their full complexity at the Glacier Metal Company, just as they are experienced in other industrial concerns. They led to an attempt to find a definition of work in the sense of work that is paid for, and a more satisfactory yardstick for measuring work directly and objectively. The pages that follow will outline the course taken in making this attempt. It is hoped that some of the experiences encountered and results obtained may be of value and assistance to others working in the same field. The methods for exploring and analysing the work content of jobs have shown evidence of practical value not only in comparing jobs but also in studying any particular form of organization in relation to the work it has been set up to do. The instruments for measuring work derive directly from the particular method used for describing work; the scope and limits for their use are the subject of continuing exploration and study. The propositions about differentials and about wage and salary structures are put forward as an introduction to a line of thought that may lead to a means of analysing work, payment, and individual capacity within a common frame of reference.

PART II

The Glacier Experience

CHAPTER II

The Problem of Status and Salaries

I

At the time the present work on status and payment was started in 1952, the status arrangements in the Glacier Metal Company were as follows.

The Company was divided into four main status groups—three grades of staff and the fourth group comprising the hourly-rated members. In its London factories (in which the present work has mainly been carried out) there were fifty members of Grade I Staff, made up mainly of divisional managers, departmental managers, and other senior personnel; and roughly one hundred and twenty members of Grade II Staff, made up of departmental superintendents, senior secretarial staff, and leading technical and office personnel. There were just under four hundred Grade III Staff personnel. This category, which was particularly heterogeneous in make-up, included all office and clerical workers (junior clerical staff as well), some office supervisors, all so-called supervisors in the Works (including some seasoned and senior supervisors controlling twenty or thirty men), and many categories of technicians—research investigators, progress officers, cost and wages clerks, invoicing clerks, inspectors, and others. The hourly-rated members numbered about eleven hundred, ranging from machine operators and labourers to skilled craftsmen.

Certain benefits went with staff status. Grades I and II were paid on a monthly, and Grade III on a weekly, basis. The staff had a minimum of six weeks' sickness benefits, a favourable pension scheme, free tea, and a special annual bonus. Grade I and II had one week longer, and Grade III two days' longer holiday than the hourly-rated members.

Each one of these four main groupings had its own representative body. The Grade I Staff Committee had five members, the Grade II Staff Committee seven members, the Grade III Staff Committee fifteen members, and the Works Committee twenty-seven members. The three staff committees were not necessarily trade-union bodies, although they did have some trade-union members on them. The Works Committee was a completely union body, all its members being shop stewards. Union membership was required in order to be nominated for the Works Committee and in order to take part in the elections for Works Committee members. Each of the four representative bodies elected members to the Works Council as follows: one from Grade I Staff Committee, two from Grade II Staff Committee, three from Grade III Staff Committee, and seven from the Works Committee (the shop stewards' committee).

An individual's status in the Company was determined partly by his personal characteristics and partly by the job he held. There was a job schedule that prescribed the particular grade into which each job fell. About one-third of the jobs were categorized as overlapping two adjacent grades. Whether or not a person who was in one of these jobs that overlapped two grades was placed in the higher or lower grade was mainly determined by assessment in terms of personal merit. Jobs were placed in a grade in the schedule according to judgment and precedent—the basis on which they were categorized as one grade or another was neither stated nor explicitly recognized. The schedule was agreed by the Works Council, and any modifications in the level of a job had to be agreed by the

Council. In the absence of principle on which the level of jobs could be determined, placing a job in a particular category, or changing its category, could be a matter of argument.

Movement from a lower to a higher grade was considered as promotion. The procedure by which a member was promoted in this way was for his manager to recommend him for upgrading. This recommendation would eventually come before the Managing Director and his immediate subordinates in the case of promotion from Grade II to I, and before a General or Divisional Manager (one level down from the Managing Director) in the case of promotion from Grade III to II, or from hourly-rated to Grade III. The person recommended was then discussed, and consideration was given to the question of whether his promotion might arouse in others feelings of dissatisfaction expressed in such terms as: 'If Mr. A. was promoted, then why not me?'

Finally, with respect to salary, all earnings were confidential. No one knew any salaries, other than his own, and those of his own subordinates if he had any. Nor were salary brackets known. It had always been the agreed policy within the firm not to divulge any information whatever about salaries.

II

The grading system had operated for a period of about fifteen years. It had been of value in diminishing many of the uncertainties previously experienced by individuals with respect to their status. And it had greatly simplified many administrative arrangements and procedures. But it had also led to difficulties because it could not always be operated with consistency. The grade that considered itself to be most hard hit by apparent inconsistencies was Grade III. The membership of this grade of staff was felt to be so heterogeneous, and to cover such a wide range of levels, that the members could find little affinity with each other, taking the grade as a whole. Almost from its inception eight years before, the Grade III

Staff Committee had suffered repeated conflict within itself each time it was faced with the problem of how best to represent its constituents in negotiating salary levels, or in resolving general questions of their status and grading. It was in this setting that, in September 1952, the Grade III Staff Committee asked the social-analyst to work with them to discover some solution to their problems.

The heterogeneity of the grade they represented divided the Grade III Committee members most severely whenever questions of salary negotiations arose. In this situation the representatives found themselves faced with the difficult task of negotiating salaries for extremely diverse groups, and in practice such difficulties were found to be insurmountable. How, for instance, could the salaries of young clerical workers correspond in any systematic manner at all with those of experienced works supervisors whose attitude towards their salary was very much influenced by what the hourly-rated workers were earning? And how could satisfactory differentials in payment be established between the salaries received by Grade III Staff members and the wages of hourly-rated operators—when the Grade III average earnings reflected such a wide range of individual salary levels? As a result of such problems, the Grade III Staff Committee was constantly faced by the question, 'What is Grade III Staff?' And no easy answer was forthcoming.

The Committee members were certain that they could resolve their problem if they could discover objective criteria for defining and measuring the responsibilities attaching to jobs—considered apart from the capacities of individual occupants of the job. Such criteria, they considered, would lay the basis for a more rational grading system built out of categories of jobs carrying similar degrees of responsibility and authority. From a grading structure of this kind, they thought that they could achieve a more rational and less troublesome salary structure.

Individual and group discussions with the Committee members provided a comprehensive picture of their attitude towards their own work and pay, and towards the grading system, the salaries structure, and the methods of payment. Their desire for changes in the methods of promotion and of re-grading individuals was also revealed. The stumbling-block was to establish criteria with which to assess degrees of responsibility and authority. The Committee had tried to use such criteria as numbers of subordinates, amount and type of equipment controlled, and amount of training or professional qualification required. But these aspects of work had proved to be of little help in comparing research, accounting, line management, production engineering, and other types of job, with their great variations in the extent to which subordinates, or equipment, or professional qualifications had anything whatever to do with them.

Rating scales and similar quasi-objective methods traditionally used for job evaluation had proved to be of no more help. These scales required judgment to select not only the particular qualities of a job to be rated, but also the weight to be given to different qualities required. The Committee members found themselves in the same dilemma—as far as objectivity was concerned—as they were in when they simply made an intuitive judgment about the whole job in the first place. Comparisons between jobs remained a matter of opinion.

III

Four months passed, and nothing much was accomplished, other than to establish that the problems experienced by the Committee would inevitably recur if they continued to use the criteria they usually used for comparing one job with another. In order to get a more positive grip on the problem, the social-analyst turned to an examination of the financial arrangements governing the social relationships under consideration. By this means, many clues can often be found about the patterns of social organization. Because of the material consequences involved, the financial aspects of social relationships tend to be regulated in a manner that reflects the realities of the situation.

Examination of the pattern of financial arrangement led to the attention of the Committee members and the social-analyst being attracted by a very familiar fact: earnings may be expressed in terms of a number of different periods of time —it being broadly true that the higher-level jobs have their salaries expressed in longer time periods than the subordinate jobs. Thus, hourly-rated members had their earnings expressed on the basis of an hourly rate; Grade III Staff members, a weekly rate; Grade II Staff members, a monthly or annual rate; and Grade I Staff members—that is to say, higher management—an annual rate.

Moreover, in certain respects the time periods seemed to be related to the 'size' of the job. Thus, for instance, the longer the period in terms of which a person's salary is expressed, the longer period of notice he must give if he resigns. Equally, the longer the period of notice he must be given to be dismissed. Consideration of these relations suggested the obvious notion that the more senior the position the longer it takes for an organization to get a new member settled into and fully occupying that position. A new hourly-paid member (with the skills for the job) may be well at work in a matter of hours; a new monthly-salaried member (also with the necessary skills) may take many months to get settled. Furthermore, this notion that it takes longer for members to get settled in more senior positions is readily connected with the equally familiar fact that the more senior positions are connected with what are commonly described as the 'long-term' as against the 'short-term' responsibilities.

The conclusion presented itself that there might be a measurable relationship between 'size' of responsibility and the time over which it is carried. Members of the Committee thought they might be on the track of a possible measure of responsibility. The first problem was to find a means of specifying the span of time of the responsibility in a job. To this end, a further series of discussions about their work was arranged.

The results of the new series of discussions were very striking indeed. Consideration of specific jobs showed that a time-span—as it was then called—could be calculated for a job by analysing the decisions that had to be taken. From this information could be discovered the maximum length of time the decisions made by a person on his own initiative committed resources of the Company. This rough and ready definition (a more comprehensive one will be given in the next chapter) proved to be quite usable from the start, despite the fact that the time-span idea was quite unfamiliar to everyone. The findings for the Committee showed maximum time-spans ranging from a week to a few months.

IV

Finding themselves in possession of a notion that, if perhaps not the measuring instrument they were looking for, at least gave some promise of being a basis on which such an instrument could be developed, the Grade III Staff Committee decided that the issue had grown sufficiently large for them to engage the attention of their Grade I and Grade II colleagues, and of management. They explained their findings—including the preliminary definition of the time-span idea—at the April 1953 meeting of the Works Council, and proposed that an examination and analysis be made of the Company's grading system as a whole.

The proposal from Grade III was considered in due course by the other two staff committees and by the management. (The Works Committee decided to hold a watching brief for the time being. They thought that the interests of their members were not affected at that stage, although they might wish to reconsider their position later on.) Because the subject of status and grading was so very touchy, it was decided to leave the status and grading issue aside for the time being, and to make a start by first studying whether the time-span idea could in fact be used, and used objectively. For example, if a member and his manager independently assessed the member's job, would they get the same maximum time-span answer? Such a study could be carried out, without at that stage going into the question of grading at all. If the time-span notion worked, there would then be time to consider what to do next.

To forward this study, each of the members of the staff committees personally volunteered to examine his own job. There were twenty-five members in all. The procedure adopted was for the analyst to have individual discussions with each of these members with a view to analysing their jobs in terms of maximum time-span. Then, at each member's request, he would obtain an independent assessment by repeating the analysis of the member's job in discussion with his manager—provided that the manager was agreeable to taking part in the discussions. Thus, it would be discovered whether the member could assign a maximum time-span to his responsibilities, whether his manager could do so, and whether there was any consistency in the results.

The results of this exploration were reported to the Works Council in the following terms in September 1953:

> On the basis of information now released by three Staff Committees, it is possible to state the following two findings from the preliminary study of time-span:
>
> (a) all members were able to describe their responsibility in terms of maximum time-span, and in a manner absolutely consistent with the independent assessment of their managers;
>
> (b) the distribution of Grade I time-spans was higher than Grade II, which was higher in turn than Grade

III. There was some overlap between Grade II and Grade I.

These results established pretty conclusively the fact that the maximum time-span attaching to jobs could be measured. Each member taking part was readily able to calculate a maximum time-span for his job. There was no dubiety. There might be some initial difficulty in coming to grips with just what decisions he was actually authorized to take. But the consideration of responsibilities in terms of the period of time that resources were committed by decisions was stated to be of great help in defining responsibilities that had not been clearly specified.

V

The results of this preliminary exploration and their own personal experiences in assessing their own jobs led the staff committee members to the conclusion that the time-span notion might prove to be of some value in studying problems of status and grading. It looked as though time might prove to be one of the important dimensions in assessing responsibility. The other dimension that at that period in the study seemed important was that of spread or breadth of responsibility—that is to say, the span of responsibility in terms of the span of topics covered. The question then facing the Works Council was what, if they were to do anything, should they do next? This question was debated in the three staff committees, and considered by the Managing Director and his immediate top management subordinates.

The consensus of opinion, strongly held, was that they should now proceed to open up the whole question, not only of status and grading, but of all the topics associated with status and grading, or lying behind the problems of status and grading. For status and grading, they clearly recognized, could not be considered apart from salaries, job titling, appointments, promotion, selection, and all aspects of the allocating of work and pay to individuals as they progressed in their careers. Therefore they might just as well recognize from the start that they would inevitably be opening up an investigation of the whole gamut of issues if they went on to an investigation of status and grading problems. As it turned out, just such a prospect was held to be most desirable. Just as much difficulty had been experienced in connection with these allied matters as with status and grading problems. Therefore, if they were possibly on the track of a means of measuring responsibility, the staff committees and management alike thought that they might most usefully and profitably carry out the development and explore the application of these measuring instruments on the broadest possible front.

Accordingly, the staff committees and management decided to go ahead with a full-scale analysis of all the matters surrounding status and grading. At the Works Council meeting in December 1953—with the Works Committee continuing to hold a watching brief—they set the following terms of reference for the continuation of the social-analysis:

(a) Further analysis of executive roles in the Company to determine whether there were gradations of responsibility and authority that could objectively be defined, and, if there were such gradations, to explore:
   (i) to what extent a *systematic ranking of executive roles emerged;* and
   (ii) whether a simple and *consistent pattern of job titling* was possible.

(b) In the light of the analysis of executive roles, to conduct a comprehensive analysis of the Company's procedures for coordinating individuals and their jobs, including:
   (i) *personal assessment and progress reporting procedures;*
   (ii) *appointment and promotion policy and procedures;*

(iii) *selection methods and procedures;*

(iv) *salary fixing and salary review principles and procedures.*

(c) Ancillary to the analysis of ranking of executive roles in terms of responsibility, to conduct *an analysis of the Company's grading system, including an analysis of the policies and procedures for according privileges on such matters as holidays, bonus, pensions, methods of payment, etc.*

Proceeding within these terms of reference, the analyst continued his work throughout the first half of 1954. Work was done individually with the members of all the three staff committees, on the basis of which reports were collated for the staff committees themselves; and discussions were conducted within the executive system. These executive discussions started with the Managing Director, and went on individually, at their request, with each of his subordinates. The results of these discussions with individuals were collated and reported to the Managing Director and his immediate subordinates jointly. Then each of the Managing Director's subordinates took the matter up independently with his own team of immediate subordinates. At their request, the analyst saw the members of this next executive layer, reporting in turn to groups comprising the manager and his immediate subordinates. This process of discussion with executive groupings was continued to the third and fourth executive layers, and in some cases went right down to the end of the executive lines in Grade III staff. In addition, members of the Association of Engineering and Shipbuilding Draughtsmen asked on their own account for a separate analysis of their jobs, in the field of production engineering, draughting, and design.

VI

The first result of the discussions within the new terms of reference was that a comprehensive picture was obtained of the wide range of problems that the analysis was intended to encompass. These initial findings were reported to the Works Council in June 1954, as a descriptive starting-point from which the further work would proceed. The problems will be very familiar to anyone who works in industry, for they are the common stuff of everyday working life.

To begin with, as already noted, there was no clear understanding of the meaning of Grades, I, II, and III. The procedure whereby some roles were rated 'Grade III or II' or 'Grade II or I' tended to cast confusion and to contribute to a feeling that a member's grade did not necessarily depend on the work he did, but depended also on his personal acceptability in the organization.

One of the effects of unclarity in the grading system was to complicate the matter of promotion. It was considered that the Company was in danger of losing good people because there was no basis on which to give them what they would feel to be an appropriate status. The frequently made comment was that a person had to change to different kinds of work in other parts of the firm in order to change in grade, because of the obscurity surrounding the possibility of promotion within the kind of work he was doing.

A further consequence of the absence of a clearly understood grading system was that individuals did not have standards against which to assess their progress in the organization. It could also lead to practices that were frowned upon, whose effects, although not intended as such, were experienced as punishment; for example, changing the title of a member's job to a title felt to carry a lower status, but leaving him with precisely the same responsibilities as he had previously held.

Because his executive authority and responsibility were coloured by a person's grading, unclarity in the grading system itself tended to reinforce unclarity in the executive organization. Questions such as, 'Who is my real manager?'

or, 'Why is my manager the same grade as I am?' were frequently raised. In similar vein, the practice of a manager having immediate subordinates of different grades was felt to be inappropriate and unrealistic.

Unclarity in the executive system led in turn to unclarity in job titling. The question of titling was one that provoked a great deal of comment. A person's title coloured his official authority because job titles were assigned to grades, and grades carried higher and lower status. But, because there was no clear and consistent use of titles, concern about status was increased. The same title (e.g. supervisor, production engineer, research assistant, office supervisor) was used to define positions that were judged to be very different in volume and character of responsibility. Job titling itself, therefore, tended to cloak differences in responsibility and authority.

With respect to payment of its members, the Company was experienced by many as implementing a policy that sometimes produced what they thought were unfair differentials. Members' responsibilities were often felt to have increased without the increase being clearly noticed so that it could be reflected in pay increases. This was held to be demonstrated by the belief that new people brought into the Company from outside to take up previously existing jobs often had to be paid at higher rates of pay than members already occupying similar jobs. And in the absence of an agreed means of measuring the degree of responsibility carried, merit review procedures were not felt to be founded on any consistent or understandable basis.

It was widely recognized, and a matter of some concern, that if a manager himself had a status and salary that were too low for the role that he occupied, then all his subordinates right down the line would tend to suffer. It was held that such a situation existed in parts of the Company, the subordinates concerned—sometimes two or three levels removed from the manager—feeling themselves to be the victims of the particular circumstance.

Finally, the findings served to demonstrate that there was no very precisely defined meaning that could be attached to work or responsibility as these terms were used in industry generally, or in the Company's own version of industrial usage. The definitions current had the serious drawback of not providing a foundation for an analysis of work from which a consistent pattern of organization could be built up. Thus, for example, resort had to be made in some parts of the Company to what was called administrative subordination, by which was meant the process of making one member subordinate to another for 'administrative purposes'. This arrangement was used as a makeshift to deal with situations in which it was quite clear to all concerned that two members, one of whom handed out work to the other, and who were thus shown on the organization chart as manager and subordinate, were really on a par with respect to the work they did. Being on a par in level of work done, they were really equal in status, both members, for example, having their work reviewed by the same manager and getting their merit increases from him. There was resulting confusion; this kind of administrative subordination turning out, in most cases, to be connected with failure to discover an appropriate type of organization for specialist jobs.

VII

One of the strongest impressions left with the social-analyst by these discussions—which, it will be recalled, were completely confidential and could not lead to any recommendations or changes being made by him—was that absolutely none of the dissatisfactions expressed with status and grading arrangements could be ascribed solely to individual disgruntlement or mere personal grievance or prejudice. In every instance, such personal dissatisfaction as did exist was found to go along with some inadequacy in organization. This connection between expressed personal dissatisfaction and practical problems of organization was observed not only in the personal views of particular individuals. It was also observable in the high degree of consistency in descriptions of the same parts of the Company by different members in their executive roles, and also by elected representatives.

It must not, of course, be concluded from the above observation that defects in organization are the only cause of dissatisfaction in individuals and that apart from the quality of organization everyone is necessarily as well adjusted in work as everyone else. But the conclusion was suggested that, on the whole, people are likely to be able to handle many of their personal difficulties by other means than precipitating them into their work situation, if the work situation is realistically organized, in the sense of giving them clear terms of reference together with a fair recognition and return for fair work done. And ineffective organization of work not only contains within it lowered efficiency, but stimulates personal dissatisfaction and encourages the bringing of resentment, envy, and other such negative feelings into work relationships.

As a summing up, and a practical extension of his impressions, the social-analyst pointed out to the Company that his experience in carrying out the study up to that point led to the conclusion that dissatisfaction with status and grading could be considered a sensitive indicator of areas in which there were shortcomings in organization; that is to say, of situations in which the work that members could get done was not commensurate with their capacity and with the effort that they had to put into the job, with resulting personal dissatisfaction and reduced Company efficiency.

CHAPTER III

The Maximum Time-Span of Discretion

I

DURING the course of the foregoing work in the first half of 1954, a more definite and precise statement of the time-span instrument was made. The use of this instrument became a central feature in the analysis of the difficulties outlined: it must therefore be described at this stage. The form in which it is presented is the form it had reached by the spring of 1955. The broad features of the instrument, however, had remained unchanged from the beginning, so that the present description is a more detailed elaboration of an instrument that, in the early stages, was employed with the assistance of a fair amount of intuitive judgment.

The method of assessment of work level for the jobs of staff members could be summarized thus: first, tease out the discretionary content of the work allocated to a particular job; second, discover the mechanisms employed to review the use of discretion by a member doing the job; third, discover the maximum period of time that would elapse under the particular conditions of review, during which the member was authorized and expected to exercise discretion on his own account in discharging the responsibilities allocated to him.

This instrument required a specification of the following main points: how to discriminate between the discretionary content of a job and its non-discretionary, or prescribed, content; and how to determine the mechanisms by which a manager reviewed his subordinate's use of discretion, and so controlled the period of time over which the subordinate used discretion on his own account.

We shall consider each of these main points in turn.

II

The *prescribed* content of a job consisted of those elements of the work about which the member was left no authorized choice. These prescribed elements were of two kinds: the result expected; and the limits set on the means by which the work could be done. Results were always prescribed in the sense that the object of a person's work was always set by his manager and not by himself. He was instructed to do this or that—to type letters, to get out a series of estimates, to design a machine tool. The letters, or estimates, or machine tool, were not left to his choice—it was some specified letter, or estimate, or machine tool that was required.

As regards method of work, or how a job was to be done, part was prescribed, and part was discretionary. Choice of method could be prescribed by such means as physical limitations, administrative routines, or more general policies governing the methods to be used in pursuing the results. Examples of such limiting factors were: the prescribed use of various types of jigs, tools, and fixtures; standardized drawings or forms on which data were entered according to predetermined schedules; routines governing the getting-out of weekly and monthly financial returns, the payment of wages, or indenting for supplies; general policies governing, say, the payment of sickness benefits, or the direction of development and research work.

The *discretionary* content of work consisted of all those elements in which choice of how to do a job was left to the person doing it. That is to say, the member doing the work was required, authorized, and expected to use discretion or judgment as he proceeded with his work, overcoming obstacles by picking what he considered the best of the alternative courses available at each stage, and pursuing the course he had chosen. Discretion was brought into play when the character of the work itself and the routines governing how the work was to be done did not automatically determine for the member doing the job the best way to do it in every respect. Some examples of discretionary content were: being left to decide what experiments to do, and how to do them, in order to carry forward a piece of research; having to choose the best feeds and speeds for an improvised job on a machine; having to decide whether the finish on a piece of work would satisfy some particular customer; having to choose from among several possible methods of manufacture in providing an estimate of cost; having to plan and organize one's work in order to get it done within a prescribed time.

If, as the analysis had suggested, it was solely the discretionary content of work that entered into what was experienced as level of work, the felt intractability of the problem of establishing realistic and satisfactory differentials became more understandable. *For the discretionary content of work was often its least evident feature. To the extent that a person was capable of doing his job, and was experienced at it, he tended not to perceive that he was using judgment or exercising discretion.* To the experienced person, and to his superior, judgment and discretion came naturally and were taken for granted. They were simply a matter of doing one's job. Conscious effort was required in scrutinizing the content of work done in order to become aware of when judgment and discretion were being used.

When taking up new responsibilities, however, a person

became painfully aware of the judgment and discretion required. Apart from the learning of routines, there was what was experienced as getting used to the job, or getting the hang of it. The manager of a new member was also suddenly made acquainted again with the amount of judgment and discretion the work he was allocating called for on the part of his subordinate. With an experienced man on the job, he could easily overlook and forget these features. When an experienced man was replaced by a newcomer, the effects of the absence of judgment and discretion soon obtruded and made themselves felt.

III

The methods a manager employed to review his subordinate's use of discretion could be divided into two main categories: direct review of work by a superior (or by someone acting on his behalf); and indirect review through the medium of reports on the effectiveness of work done reaching the superior from sources outside his direct control. In order to discover these review mechanisms, it was necessary to analyse how work done was controlled in terms of the mechanisms that would come into play should a member use consistently bad discretion at a marginal level. That is to say, a search was made for the methods by which a manager would discover, not the serious errors of judgment—these were usually easy to detect—but errors of judgment of such a degree as cumulatively to have economically significant effects, but individually not to attract attention unless looked for. Such an approach to the analysis of control mechanisms highlighted the fact that, in ordinary circumstances, members who were carrying out a job did not use bad discretion. Therefore, the effects that could arise from marginally bad discretion had to be worked out, in order to perceive the review mechanisms that would be brought into play, but most often went completely unrecognized.

Direct review of work occurred when the results of the work done were surveyed by a superior in such a way that all discretionary aspects were scrutinized. The survey could be made by an inspector or by some other specialist acting for him and under his control. In analysing direct review mechanisms, great care was required not to mistake an apparent review for an actual one, and conversely not to overlook review mechanisms that existed but were not noticed. For example, it was found that a superior receiving from a subordinate a monthly report on that subordinate's work was not necessarily carrying out a review each month. If the subordinate was himself allowed to choose what he thought was significant and ought to be reported, and to omit what he judged to be proceeding satisfactorily and hence to need no comment, then a review was not taking place. If, however, he was making a detailed report according to a schedule laid down by his superior, which his superior then surveyed, a review was being made. Thus, a superior inspecting a drawing made by a subordinate would be reviewing his work if he went through the drawing so as to check each point at which discretion was allowed; but he was not making a review if he merely scrutinized the drawing to ensure that the general features of the design were correct, but left unchecked the many details that called for the use of discretion within the general terms of reference. A full review of work was not necessarily implied in an Annual General Meeting considering a report from its Board of Directors and Managing Director; nor in a manager's counter-signature on a document prepared by a subordinate; nor in a foreman's passing of a job of work completed by a craftsman. Many discretionary elements of the work done might not necessarily have been subjected to scrutiny at that time. The sole issue at stake was whether the full, authorized discretion had been reviewed, and this could only be determined by examination of the facts in each actual case.

Indirect review mechanisms were found to come into play when the work done by a member next moved, unreviewed, to someone outside the line of command of the member's superior; for instance, when work was delivered to a customer, or orders were sent to a supplier, or services were provided to other members of the organization or were requested from them. The manager could only check the discretion used by his subordinate—where, of course, discretion was allowed—by means of incoming favourable reports or complaints, or the absence of complaints.

The assessment of discretion by indirect means required investigation of the specific period elapsing before the effects of the discretion used could be brought to the attention of the member's superior. Thus, in the case of some estimating jobs, unreviewed use of discretion could occur during the weeks that might elapse before the estimates returned in the form of customers' orders so that they could be checked by a planning engineer. In some senior inspection jobs there was the authority to use discretion in deciding whether the quality of work was within the limits required by a specific customer. This discretion could be checked only in the light of customer returns, which might not happen until several months had passed. During these months it was possible that other finished goods had been piling up in stock before being delivered all at once.

With these indirect reviews, it was found, reports reached a member's superior in gradually increasing number. The superior could keep to a minimum the time-span of discretion he allowed to his subordinate, by reviewing each report as it came back. Or he could increase the time-span by not reviewing each report, but rather by noting general trends in the reports received. It was observable that as a superior gained increasing confidence in a subordinate, he turned to reviewing work on the basis of the trend of results, and was not worried by isolated, seemingly bad reports occurring from time to time. It may readily be appreciated, however, that this switch in the character of the review mechanism could go unnoticed, with the result that the increase in level of work being allocated would pass unnoticed. Intuitive judgment would often, in these circumstances, lead to merit increases in payment being awarded, but the rationale for the increase remained obscure, because on the surface it appeared that the same job was being done.

IV

The time-span method for describing and measuring the level of work in a job was experienced as unfamiliar and strange by members of the Company when they worked with it for the first time. It required a separation in thought between *description of type* of job, and *measurement of size* of job. Type of job was traditionally described in terms of the prescribed results; e.g. a typist, estimator, supervisor, draughtsman. This description and titling worked very well if it was taken no further. But trouble did arise when these titles were taken as telling something more—something about the size of a job—by virtue of stereotyped notions about the importance of the work of a typist, or an estimator, or a supervisor, or a draughtsman, and about the salary bracket and status that should go along with such work. These stereotypes were clung to, because it was the prescribed content of a job, including both the routines and results expected, that was often its seemingly most important or dramatic aspect.

The prescribed content of work was often complex and difficult to learn. Years of training might be spent acquiring the routines for carrying out the prescribed aspects of jobs so that all possibility of mistake was removed. For example, there were those jobs concerned with accuracy in transferring entries from one data sheet to another in accordance with prescribed but detailed schedules—ledgers, sales cards, drawings, layouts. Descriptions of such jobs usually laid great stress upon the great responsibility they carried for accuracy and reliability. The possible consequences of carelessness and mistakes could be very serious indeed. From the point of view of discretionary content, however, these prescribed features might recede completely into the background. The responsibility of the person in such a job could be solely that of organizing and controlling the pace of his work, so as not to fall behind, during the time he was left working on his own.

When they gave careful consideration to the matter, members of the Company came quite independently to the same conclusion: the prescribed content of work could not be used as an index of size of job, and if it was so used it inevitably led to trouble. The reason why prescribed content was found to be useless, and misleading, as a measure was that failure to conform to prescribed methods and results could only come about through a mistake, through carelessness, negligence, or dishonesty. And there was no way of establishing the consequences of such behaviour. Anything from negligible to disastrous consequences might follow. Even in the very simplest of jobs it was possible to cause very damaging or dangerous happenings through clumsiness or mistakes or negligence—as, say, a watchman who neglected his rounds, or a machinist who dropped a spanner into a fragile and easily damaged machine that was essential for production, or a clerk who put a decimal point in the wrong place.

When they examined jobs in other industries, they found that the same state of affairs seemed to hold. They obtained support for their finding that the determination of relative status of jobs, or differentials in pay, was completely unrealistic if based upon comparisons of the prescribed aspects of jobs. Thus, many functions having to do with protection against loss of life were most often prescribed functions, such as safety precautions in the working of dangerous equipment and processes. Or, to take an example far removed from Glacier, there were the complex routines and systems controlling the movement of passenger trains, which left nothing affecting the lives of passengers to the *discretion* of those actually operating the signalling system or running the trains. Payment for such jobs, however emotionally argued in terms of prescribed functions, was never argued in terms of payment that in any sense at all matched the consequences of failure to follow regulations in carrying out these functions. It seemed evident that society did not expect its members to be negligent, or to make mistakes, or to be dishonest. Or, at least, society did not appear to offer differential rewards for degrees of honesty, or degrees of carefulness, or degrees of avoidance of negligence.

V

Despite very conscious awareness that it led only to confusion to bring prescribed elements of jobs into consideration of level of work, members of the Company nevertheless found it difficult to stop doing so. They were pretty strongly attached to the use of these prescribed elements. A great deal of emotion was aroused at the thought that such factors as accuracy, reliability, honesty, knowledge of routine procedures, number of subordinates, degree of skill required, formal qualifications possessed, might not prove to be of much account in assessing level of work. The importance of such factors had been popularly subscribed to for many years.

Because of the very strong emotions almost automatically aroused, a very considerable effort of will was required to change to a new frame of reference, in which the size of job was considered only in terms of the discretion exercised in doing the job, leaving the more familiar prescribed results out of account except to specify the type of work. Such a procedure was in sharp contrast to the description of work in terms of prescribed content, which allowed reference to be made to whole categories of jobs all at once under the same title—even though it was granted that difficulties might result from doing this. The effort required to adjust to the new frame of reference was increased by the fact that the discovery of discretionary content and review mechanisms required hard and painstaking work. It could not be determined by mere superficial scrutiny. Generalized statements, over-simplified statements, suppositions—none of these would substitute for accurate description of discretionary requirements and the actuality of review mechanisms.

It was the concrete reality of the specific job that was the starting point. If one job was to be compared with another, then the actual work in each of the jobs in terms of the discretion required had to be compared, and not the titles of the jobs, or activities that, although identical in appearance, were discretionary in one job and prescribed in another.

Moreover, the new frame of reference meant that a favourite and well-established technique of arguing about jobs had to be given up. This was the technique of reference to hypothetical jobs to bolster up an argument in favour of giving greater weight to some characteristic or other that someone might consider to be especially important. This technique was often used in trying to assess the time-span notion. Thus, for example, the job of captain of a large ocean liner crossing the Atlantic might be cited as showing how a very responsible job could have a time-span of only five days—the time taken to make each crossing—if it were supposed, for the purpose of discussion, that the captain's work was reviewed at the end of each crossing. Such a supposition might appear reasonable enough at first sight. But no job can be discovered in reality that conforms to it. The responsibilities in such jobs include the administration of a large staff, planning of maintenance, and all the other duties required in the year-in, year-out running of a large undertaking; the maximum time-span of such responsibilities may run into some years.

The method of assessing work in terms of discretion also ran headlong into the common idea that many jobs required no use of discretion at all in their performance; they were purely routine or automatic. *In practice, no such job has been found.* Nor is it likely that such a job exists, or ever will exist. Every job has some discretion in it, even though the discretion might not be apparent to those who do not know the job, or might seem too insignificant to those who do. A person's rate of work is one factor that remains discretionary, even though other aspects of the job are standardized. When jobs are standardized to the point of becoming automatic, they are made automatic. No one would, or could, do them. The paradoxical effect is that the job may then produce a new and greater discretionary responsibility—that of running the automatic machine. To say, therefore, about any job that it requires no discretion is a gross error. The discretionary content is there, and requires only to be discovered. It has been noticed that the discretionary content of a job is usually pretty unfamiliar to anyone but the person doing it, or his manager.

Experience of discussion with members showed that it was possible to think up all sorts of jobs that on the surface appeared feasible, but simply did not exist in reality. And much confusion about the time-span notion always ensued when such hypothetical jobs were used as examples. But there still remained the question, was it worth the effort to change to a new way of looking at work? Was the time-span not merely one dimension of size of job, the other dimensions being so difficult to calculate that the use of time-span made things no better? These were the questions studied during the succeeding phase of the analysis.

CHAPTER IV

Analysis of Status and Salary Problems

I

BY the end of 1954, interviews had been conducted with about 300 members of the Company individually and in groups. These interviews—the results of which the social-analyst had been authorized to use in his reports to the Works Council—had been arranged by the Staff Committee members, by the Association of Engineering and Shipbuilding Draughtsmen's Branch, by managers concerned with specific problems of organization, and by individual members with a personal interest in time-span and ranking. From these interviews had come an analysis of their views of their own jobs and, in some cases, of subordinate jobs—about 450 in all—covering practically every type of work done in the Company: manufacturing, sales, research, production engineering, drawing and design, estimating, planning, production control, costing, accounting and invoicing, building maintenance, civil engineering, inspection, purchasing and dispatch, personnel, training, and secretarial.

The detailed analyses of individual jobs reinforced the previous finding that the time-spans of jobs could be measured. But they did more than that. They gave evidence that the use of time-span of discretion for measuring work might lead to a new and different perception of salary and status problems, so that they could be settled in a manner that took into account the changes and fluctuations always occurring as a result of changes in work, or in people, or in negotiated wage levels.

II

In the earlier exploratory studies, it had been found that the higher the grade, and, in general terms, the higher the executive level, the higher was the time-span. This finding was reinforced by the additional finding that positions in the same line of command showed descending time-spans as the analysis proceeded from superior to subordinate positions. On reflection, it became apparent that this latter finding must inevitably obtain: a manager simply could not work within a shorter time framework than his subordinates; the period of his discretionary freedom must encompass the periods within which his subordinates worked, since he allocated the work and held his subordinates to account.

To note that in general terms time-span and executive level were related was, however, a far cry from suggesting that the maximum time-span of discretion might itself be a measure of level of work. But the possibility of just such a connection thrust itself forward as a result of regular relationship between maximum time-span and salary—a relationship that manifested itself with increasingly dramatic force as more and more positions were analysed. These results were observed in the following manner, at a time when the social-analyst and staff members were still working with the idea in mind that time-span was but one dimension of a complex measure of work, the other dimensions of which were unknown.

In the course of interviews with members, the question of the salaries they were paid was often raised. The social-analyst came to learn of the earnings of many individuals. But, more important, he came to learn of the salaries that they considered would be a fair return for the work they were doing—regardless of whether they were actually earning such a salary—taking into account the salary levels obtainable elsewhere at that time in their particular field of work.

From these data, the following important relationship was noted: *members whose work carried the same maximum time-span of discretion, whatever their field of work, were found to state—with only slight variations—the same salary as being a fair return, at the general rates then obtaining, for the work they were doing.* Thus, for example, of eight members whose work was established by themselves and their managers to carry a maximum time-span of one month, all, quite independently, stated practically identical sums of money—about £12.10s.—as salaries that would satisfy them as being a fair return for their work. The degree of consistency could be illustrated by the fact that four members stated about £12.10s. and the other four stated amounts ranging from £12 to £13 per week. These replies, moreover, came from members working in extremely diverse occupations.

The findings held true at whatever level of work the comparisons were made, as outlined in the accompanying table.[1] Each person—accountant, engineer, research technician,

Maximum Time-Span	Expected Earnings (April 1954)
One hour	£8. 0s. p.w.
One day	£9. 0s. p.w.
One week	£10.10s. p.w.
One month	£12.10s. p.w.
One year	£980 p.a.
Two years	£2,000 p.a.

[1] These figures were not reported to the firm at that time. Publication of actual figures was eventually agreed in July 1955. See p. 79.

supervisor—expected the same return for the same maximum time-span of responsibility. It appeared as though there existed in people's minds a pattern of rates expected for level of work done, and that this pattern was made manifest by stating level of work in maximum time-span terms.

A practical test for the possible existence of a pattern of rates expected for given levels of work was carried out in subsequent interviews. The first significant finding was that where there were individual grievances about salary, these were associated with payment below the rate ordinarily expected for the time-span at which the member was working. Members who were paid at the expected level were satisfied with their pay, in the sense of regarding themselves as getting a fair return for what they did—although this, of course, in no way precluded their favouring or indeed working for a general salary increase to improve everyone's position without changing the levels of individuals relative to each other.

Moreover, the social-analyst began to find that, as his work progressed, he was able to estimate the salaries of members with increasing accuracy. Once the maximum time-span of a member's work was established, it only remained to learn whether the member considered he was getting a fair return for his work. Then by reference to the salary ordinarily expected for that level of work, it was possible to state to within 5 per cent what the member was in fact earning.

Whatever level of work (or degree of responsibility, or size of job) might mean, if it were at all connected with people's assessment of fair pay, then the evidence was highly suggestive that maximum time-span was a measure of the level.

III

Supporting the emergence of a possible pattern of rates of pay for level of work as evidence that maximum time-span might itself be a measure of level of work, was the existence of what appeared to be a systematic pattern of ranks or levels, connected with the executive organization, which could be observed by reference to time-span.

Cross-reference between positions showed that members tended to group them in categories in a consistent manner. Thus, for example, of three positions at, say, three-week, five-week, and six-month time-span levels, the five-week and six-month time-span positions were felt by the members as having an affinity in status. The three-week-level position was experienced by all three members as being in a junior category, although mathematically the three-week and five-week positions were closer. In this fashion, groupings were found for jobs of time-span up to one hour; between one hour and one day; one day and a week; one week and one month; one month and one year; one year and two years; two years and five years; and over five years.

The boundaries between the categories at the one-month level and above were experienced as firmer boundaries than those below the one-month level. The main reason for this appeared to be that no positions at lower than one-month level of work were found to carry full managerial authority and responsibility—that is to say, authority over subordinates in the sense of selecting them, assessing their work, dealing with their salary increases, and in all respects being managerially in charge of them. The Company could be described as comprising five executive ranks, the lowest ranks composed of three sub-ranks. The shortest possible executive line between Managing Director and the shop floor would comprise the Managing Director at the over-five-year level, a subordinate in the two- to five-year category, one in the one- to two-year category, one in the one-month to one-year category, and finally a subordinate in one of the sub-categories of less than a month.

The other feature of these categories was that whereas increase in time-span of work within a rank was primarily experienced as an increase in work, movement across one of the boundaries was felt not just as increase in work but as promotion. This promotion was perceived as moving from the top of one category to the bottom of the next, from a ceiling in earnings to the possibility once again of moving up a bracket. Thus, movement over the one-month boundary meant movement into the managerial area. Similarly, movement across each of the succeeding boundaries was experienced as movement into a higher managerial region.

IV

It was taken as a working basis from the foregoing that the firm had been applying, without knowing it, a systematic pattern of salaries and of ranks—a pattern that could be observed once level of work was measured by time-span. But because this pattern was unrecognized, it could not be used effectively as a conscious aid to planning; and divergences from the pattern, although intuitively felt as such, could not be readily pin-pointed or defined as such. Such conclusions, and the conclusion that the maximum time-span of discretion authorized in a job was a measure of the level of work allocated, could, of course, be only tentative. It became increasingly apparent that these conclusions could not readily be tested in any absolute sense. For there always remained the difficult question of just what were the particular elements of a job that were experienced by people as work—in the sense of the work that carried status and financial reward.

It seemed more profitable, therefore, to ask not whether time-span was an absolute measure of level of work, but rather what sort of analysis was possible if it was assumed that time-span did measure level of work. The following sections present the picture that emerged when the matter was dealt with in this manner—using the time-span instrument as a tool for analysing those problems of status and payment (described in an earlier chapter) experienced by staff members.

V

Among the main sources of difficulty were the changes that were always going on to some extent, affecting different parts of the firm in different ways and at different times. These changes were of three main kinds. First, changes in both the type of work and the level of work done by the firm. These changes occurred as a result of changes in market requirements or of new developments in production, or of a general expansion or contraction of the firm. Second, changes in the individuals making up the firm. These changes occurred either through changes in the capacity of those members already employed or through changes in personnel because of labour turnover. And third, changes in levels of payment. These changes occurred on account of negotiated national or local awards or changes in the value of money and in the cost of living. The effect of these continually occurring fluctuations and changes in work, personnel, and payment was to subject the Company's organization to pressures that could disturb it and set it askew.

Such changes were the more disturbing when they went unrecognized. Changes whose occurrence was not perceived could not be subjected to conscious planning. Such changes tended to be recognized from the symptoms produced after they had taken place. These symptoms were quite familiar. For example, an unrecognized upward change in level of work across the boundary of a rank would eventually cause members to be dissatisfied with their status and salary, should they perform satisfactorily at the new level; or members would experience increasing difficulty in discharging their responsibilities, for no very apparent reason, because of the unrecognized promotion that had taken place into jobs with significantly greater demands on them than had previously obtained. Conversely, an unrecognized downward change in level of work across the boundary of a rank would cause members to be dissatisfied with the work they were given to do, and would create a feeling of a 'closing of the gap' in comparison with the earnings in more junior positions.

When analysed in terms of levels of work, one of the common circumstances found to precipitate status and salary problems was that of concurrent changes in work level and in the capacity of individuals. An accumulation of isolated upward changes in the level of work of a particular type, which corresponded with advance in capacity of some of the members, led to these members quite automatically being given and assuming the new levels of work of that type without being aware of it. Eventually, should the advance in level of work cross the boundary into the next rank, and the members develop to the point where they could continue to do the work, the conditions were set for creating within the manager's command positions with levels of work similar to his own. And all this could remain unrecognized because, after all, there were still the same people, with the same titles, doing the same type of work.

As a consequence of such circumstances, the members became more like colleagues than subordinates of their manager, a fact that was in conflict with their job titles and organizationally subordinate positions. Such a situation was experienced as difficult both by the members concerned and by their immediate colleagues. With respect to payment, there did not seem to be hope of fair assessment for any of them. For the members at the higher levels of work were considered as being at the top salary for their work as perceived, whereas, taking into account their true level of work, they ought actually to have moved to the bottom of the next higher bracket. And, as for some of their colleagues, their salaries might be held down, because their work was compared with the work done by the 'better' members and their pay was set accordingly.

Difficulties produced by unrecognized changes in the level of work being done were reacted to just as strongly by the managers as by subordinates. The task of merit assessment and assignment of proper status was made very difficult and tenuous. Grievances about salary and status might crop up frequently enough to be disruptive of work and to produce an uneasy feeling—about which it did not seem much could be done—that there were underlying difficulties not being coped with. It also became an arduous task, and sometimes a seemingly profitless one, to try to maintain a sound organization without a yardstick to help in recognizing and measuring work levels.

Changes such as those described are part of the ordinary daily happenings in any organization. In addition, however, the Company had gone through a post-war phase of expanding its activities and laying the basis for actual expansion in size. In this phase it had purchased a small aluminium die-casting firm; the main Scottish factory had been doubled in size; the firm's service stations in Manchester and Glasgow had been increased in size and in range of work done; and in addition to the manufacture of new lines of bearings, they had started the manufacture and sale of a centrifugal oil filter. The significance of these developments had been partially catered for by a managerial reorganization at top level; the full extent of the change became more clearly manifest, however, when the effects on level of work in positions at all levels in the Company were assessed.

It was noted, first, that the positions of Managing Director and his subordinates had increased considerably in level of work—an increase great enough to raise these positions one rank in level. Members who had remained in those roles that had increased in rank had in effect—and in reality—been promoted. They had bigger jobs to fill.

There had been accompanying upward pulls in level of work in various jobs throughout the organization. These upward pulls had been dealt with to a very great extent by a radical reorganization of the Company's total executive structure, which took three years to accomplish in broad outline. This big achievement had, however, left many detailed difficulties in its wake—in particular, difficulties in establishing levels of work, and hence status and salary, for some of the new or modified jobs. As a result, an imbalance had occurred in some sections where some of the positions had advanced to the next rank in level of work, and others had not. Failure to recognize such situations and to bring about the reorganization required could be seen to add to their status and grading problem; and it interfered with conscious plans and decisions aimed at stepping up the efficiency with which their work was done.

VI

Some of the remaining matters that had been raised in the course of the exploration were analysed in the following way.

A. As the analysis progressed, it became possible to discern changes in the financial values assigned by members to levels of work. The cost of living had been increasing and the hourly-rated members had received two national wage awards. As these changes occurred, it was noticeable in discussions that the salary levels mentioned in connection with given levels of work gradually increased. It was as though the various members had discussed the matter among themselves, and agreed a new policy with respect to the salary appropriate to given time-span levels. Thus, for example, during November 1953, £625 per annum was cited as a fair salary by members working at the one-month time-span level. By April 1954, the figure had changed to £650. Then, several months later, other members at this level of work gave £675 as a fair return. So, during a period of two years, the figure was observed to move from the original sum of £625 to a sum of £725 in February 1955. The salaries cited for other levels moved upwards in the same systematic way—the general pattern of salaries being maintained intact—as illustrated in the accompanying diagram.[1]

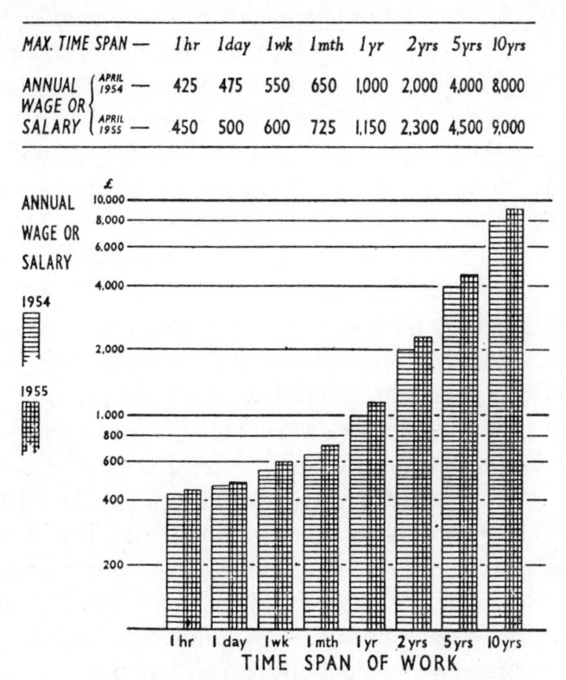

MAX. TIME SPAN —		1 hr	1 day	1 wk	1 mth	1 yr	2 yrs	5 yrs	10 yrs
ANNUAL WAGE OR SALARY	APRIL 1954 —	425	475	550	650	1,000	2,000	4,000	8,000
	APRIL 1955 —	450	500	600	725	1,150	2,300	4,500	9,000

This movement in the pattern of salaries experienced as fair return for level of work done, offered strong evidence that there were very general and intuitively sensed notions about work and pay.[2] The likelihood was that one of the most important factors giving rise to and supporting this intuitive

[1] Some of the data for this diagram (particularly the higher time-span figures) have been obtained from other industrial concerns besides the Glacier Metal Company.

[2] A possible connection between these figures and the changes in the index of industrial production has been pointed out by Mr. J. M. M. Hill. The increases in the above figures range between 16 per cent and 25 per cent. The index of industrial production rose between December 1953, and March 1955, from 121 to 141, an increase of 16 per cent. The possibility suggests itself that the pressures towards true pay increases are closely attuned to productivity, although, of course, these data are insufficient for any definite conclusions.

grasp of the value of work was that of labour turnover—new members joining and old members leaving the Company. A second factor was that of testing other jobs by reading advertisements and even applying for them to find out more about them. There was also the opportunity for members to compare their own value and the value of their jobs with other members and other jobs, and to judge how they stood. By all accounts, these judgments appeared to be shrewdly and accurately made by persons, in their inner minds at least, whatever they might consciously have recognized, or openly acknowledged to others.

B. Recognition of level of work in jobs, and of change in level, was necessary in order to gain control over circumstances where a member was advancing in personal capacity, but where the level of work available to him in his particular occupation remained static, or perhaps decreased. Either the member could find or be found work at a satisfactory level elsewhere in the firm, or the likelihood was that he would eventually leave and seek work elsewhere—unless, of course, he chose to remain in work at a level below the full level of his capacity. Where there had been failure to recognize the situation, pressure would build up to the point where the member might leave unexpectedly and with a sense of grievance.

What was regarded as an equally serious situation was the danger of losing members performing work that needed to be done, but that was at a level in a higher rank than the recognized status and payment for their job. The reaction of such members tended to be that the Company did not appreciate their true worth. Their impulse was to seek employment elsewhere. This kind of situation, although perhaps not the sole cause, was nevertheless a contributing factor to the Company's losing some members it did not wish to lose. The analysis emphasized an important and difficult aspect of being a manager—that of being able to recognize when a subordinate had moved (or was moving) up into a level of work that fell within his own rank, and to secure, if possible, the eventual re-positioning of the subordinate within the organization.

C. Occasional difficulties were experienced when positions fell vacant and had to be filled from outside the Company. It might then be discovered that the vacancy could be filled only at a higher rate than had previously been paid. From management's point of view it sometimes seemed as though such rates were paid because of 'scarcity value' owing to shortages of certain types of specialist. From members' point of view they were paid because in some instances Glacier rates were too low. Filling vacancies at these higher rates gave rise to the comment that newcomers did better than those already employed. Where this type of situation was met, detailed consideration of the work content of the positions revealed that time-span—despite the job title—was at a higher level than the jobs ordinarily appearing under the title. There was usually evidence that the level of work in the job had recently been increasing as a result of new types of work being done. The person who had left the job vacant had either been underpaid, or else had not been up to the work. The salary held to be necessary because of scarcity was no more than the salary to be expected if the correct level of work in the job had been recognized. Therefore, it seemed useful to take heed of any feeling that payment for scarcity value was necessary, as a warning to examine the possibility that the vacancy was for a position of unrecognized higher level of work.

This was not to say that the need to pay for scarcity value *per se* might never arise. But no instance was encountered in the present study where scarcity value was anything more than payment for an unrecognized level of work according to the pattern revealed by time-span. What did seem to happen when there was a scarcity of a particular type of specialist, was that these specialists could command higher levels of work than they might ordinarily expect to be given, and that they received a salary in accord with this higher level of work. Thus, newly graduated University students might choose employment with a firm that offered the greatest work opportunities to start with (even though they might not eventually stay with that firm). Smaller firms, in order to compete with the long-term prospects offered by larger organizations, might have to suffer the risk of offering higher levels of work to begin with than they might otherwise have done, as inducement to attract the people they required.

D. The problems arising out of job titling, seen from the angle of level of work, required the separation of title for indicating type of work, and for indicating level of work. To the specification that a position was that of a junior estimator, a junior clerk, an assistant cost accountant, a chief electrician could be added the actual level of work in terms of the time-span of discretion in the job. A one-month time-span estimating job could thereby be distinguished from one of a three-day time-span, even though both were titled estimator. A senior draughtsman's job of three-week time-span could be distinguished from a senior clerical job of one-week time-span, even though traditional usage in the two different fields called for the use of the title 'Senior'. And the title 'Chief' as applied, say, to a position of head inspector of over one-year time-span could be distinguished from the title 'Chief' as applied to a position of charge-hand labourer with one-day time-span.

E. One of the earliest questions raised also seemed to be resolvable—the question 'What is Grade III Staff?' Analysis showed that Grade III Staff was a conglomeration of positions with levels of work of hours, days, weeks, and, in some cases, months. When those positions were taken that were pretty consistently felt by members to belong together in terms of having a common status, three main groupings emerged. When these groups were analysed in terms of time-span, a definite pattern was found: the three groups were composed of the jobs over one month, those between one week and one month, and those under one week. The members in the group of jobs above the one-month level had a greater affinity of interest with Grade II Staff and their conditions than with Grade III Staff. The members in the group of jobs between one week and one month considered themselves as the true Grade III. The under one-week jobs were considered as another grade altogether—possibly a new Grade IV.

The Grade III Staff seemed therefore to contain elements of at least three different levels, which would have to be separated if the grading system were continued. The analysis of the situation had not been completed, however, and it might be that other distinctions would appear. The experience nevertheless indicated that these distinctions were much more readily manageable and catered for given a yardstick for measuring level of work.

F. The analysis suggested that the systematic operation of ranking and salary-bracket conceptions might set a framework for dealing with changes in organization and in the position of individuals, by setting limits on the levels of work, and hence of personnel, that a manager could have immediately under his command. If the level of work in any immediately subordinate role moved either above or below the established levels of work, the position would have to be established at a higher or lower level, unless, by a redistribution of duties between several jobs, the established levels of all could be maintained. If, on the other hand, an immediately subordinate member showed himself capable of work—and hence of earning a salary—at a level outside the boundaries established for his job, this would have to be discussed with him. In due course it would be necessary to appoint him to a position at a more appropriate level if he was to be retained by the Company. Career planning for members with growing skill and capacity could become possible with greater precision than before.

VII

Once the elected representatives had analysed their own jobs in terms of time-span, the initiative for further development of the analysis came from within the executive system. By the autumn of 1954, the main emphasis in the work was upon a very widespread analysis of the level of work available in different functions in the organization. These explorations were pursued at the request of managers and their subordinates who wished to find out whether the time-span instrument would help them to get a sufficient perception of the work that they were doing and the responsibilities they were carrying to allow them to build their status and salary structure on principles that could be made explicit. In some cases, calculation of time-span was comparatively easy. Within half an hour's or an hour's discussion of the particular job, it was possible with reasonable sureness on the part of the member concerned to calculate a firm time-span for the job of work done. In other instances, it was much more difficult. Some jobs required many hours of discussion and analysis to discover the time-span content, and many difficulties were encountered. The difficulties in arriving at a time-span measure were caused by two main factors: uncertainty of members about the discretionary content of the work they were allocating or had been given to do; and uncertainty about the review mechanisms operating. In other words, difficulties in using the time-span instrument arose not so much from difficulties in the instrument itself, as from lack of clarity about the job of work being done, and it was precisely where it was found most difficult to apply that the time-span instrument was experienced as most useful. In these cases, final achievement of a measure of time-span meant that the manager and his subordinate had considerably clarified their ideas about the work being done—in some instances gaining for the first time a clear and precise picture of its real content and level.

In connection with these executive analyses, the use of the

time-span instrument has become increasingly sensitive. With this increased sensitivity a further conception has emerged—that of the *range of level of work* in each position. This is the widest range within which work can be assigned to a member in the position, from the lowest level compatible with the required job being done, to the highest level available to be assigned. Thus, for example, in a research development position, there might be available projects some of which would require up to six months to complete. These projects might be assigned at the six-month level. In such a case, the member would be expected to carry full responsibility for completing any project assigned to him without review until completion—whether large projects requiring six months to complete, or smaller projects of a shorter time-span. Or they might be assigned at lower than the six-month level to a less capable member. In such a case (say at the three-month level), the member would be expected to complete all projects up to those requiring three months. On the three- to six-month projects, however, his progress would be reviewed at intervals of three months or less during the development of his work.

The range of level of work cannot be expanded or contracted at will. The upper limit is set by the work available. At the lower limit, the point is soon reached at which any further reduction would mean so much involvement by a manager in reviewing his subordinate's work that he would have no freedom to do his own. It would be quicker for him to do the job himself. Thus, in the above example, such a bottom point might be reached at, say, the one-month level. If this were the case, the position could be described as having a range of level of work from one month to six months.

The measurement of range of level of work in a job is proving to be of considerable practical importance. It requires managers to specify the limits of the jobs under them, and lays a foundation for an open and known establishment. Such an establishment makes possible a number of practical measures. It allows maximum and minimum salary levels to be fixed on a firm basis, rather than by guess-work or past experience, for advertising and selection. The advancement of subordinates within a job can be watched; and the time when subordinates will surpass the maximum available level in their jobs can be predicted. Moreover, it allows members to know just what prospects there are in each job, so that they can take this into account in their own career planning. And it makes it easier for members to know when they are approaching the limits of the job they are in, should they wish to progress further. It may thus prevent the fruitless argument that can arise when members reach the top limit of the available work in their existing job, without this situation being readily identifiable.

VIII

Taking the results of the analysis of difficulties experienced over status and salary problems, along with the discovery of the systematic pattern of salaries and ranks that appeared to exist unrecognized, it did seem as though measuring level of work in terms of time-span might have some practical value. It was recognized, of course, that the findings described did not in any absolute sense establish that time-span measured work or responsibility. The fundamental question of what work was remained unanswered. It was still only an assumption that work was connected with the use of discretion. But not having resolved these important theoretical questions had not proved too serious a drawback. It was possible to use the time-span instrument to good effect as a means of analysing organizational, status, and salary problems, and of teasing out the various factors operating. Without some such instrument the field remained obscure and confused, because it was difficult to discern just what was happening. With the time-span description one had an instrument that seemed to give consistent explanations of what was happening.

CHAPTER V

Manual Work and the Hourly-Rated Operator

I

DURING the discussions on staff status and salaries and the reports that had been presented between December 1952 and September 1953, the Works Committee, it will be recalled, had held a watching brief. Their view had been that since it was staff grading that was involved, the hourly-rated members were not directly concerned. At the point, however, where the analysis touched on the question of staff salaries in relation to level of work done, the Works Committee reconsidered their position. If progress could be made with respect to the analysis of staff jobs, then it might be useful, they thought, to have an analysis of hourly-rated members' jobs as well. This decision was reported by the Secretary of the Works Committee to the Works Council at its meeting in September 1954. He said that the Works Committee had many problems similar to those discussed by staff, and they would like to be included in any further work done, so that the question of hourly-rated wages could be considered as well.

The difficulties experienced by the hourly-rated members arose from the fact that wage brackets had been fixed for each and every type of hourly-rated job. These wage brackets had been fixed in the course of very lengthy discussions that had taken place between shop stewards, Trade Union officials, and management. They had hammered out an agreed value for each kind of role—machinist, toolmaker, millwright, electrician, painter, packer, inspector, welder, and all the other kinds of hourly-rated work. They took the fitter's rate as the basis, as was the agreed practice in the engineering industry, and used it as the main criterion for assessing the correct wage levels in other jobs, taking into account at the same time the length of time it would take to train a man to take over the responsibilities of the particular job under consideration. These criteria of the fitter's rate and the time of training, plus intuitive judgment, had allowed a pattern of wage brackets to be established that was felt to be on the whole satisfactory, and that worked with a fair degree of effectiveness.

But the use of the wage brackets was not free of trouble. As soon as brackets were established, there arose the thorny question of the conditions under which a member could expect to be paid over the top of his bracket. The policy on which the wage brackets were based stated that members could be paid above the top level of their bracket if they showed evidence of exceptional ability. In practice it turned out that exceptional ability was extremely difficult to define. Its definition could be a source of considerable argument between a manager, an hourly-rated member, and his shop steward representative. Along the same lines, there arose the question of the standards to be used in promoting an operator from one bracket to another, when there was a series of brackets covering the same kind of job carried out at different levels. This situation applied in particular to machine operators, for whom there were four brackets—A, B, C, and D—ranging from the machine operators who were at the bottom of the A bracket, to the very highly skilled machinists at the top of the D bracket. Various criteria were used, such as flexibility, versatility, high degree of skill, capacity to work to very fine tolerances, capacity to do many different kinds of work, capacity to do one particular kind of work extremely well, cooperativeness, and willingness. The difficulty with these various criteria was that in many instances they were mutually contradictory. For example, promotion could be expected either for versatility or for being extremely good at one specialized job; the conditions, however, under which either versatility or specialization were to apply could not be defined in any systematic way so that a principle could be elaborated that could be used with consistency.

A further difficulty arose over members who were able to do jobs appearing in different categories. For example, there might be one wage bracket for a storeman and another for a fork truck driver. How was the work of a man who was used both as storeman and as fork truck driver to be calculated? And finally, there was the problem of what to do when it was felt that a given wage bracket no longer fitted the circumstances of the work. In the absence of general principles, changing a wage bracket was a difficult step to take. An apparently obvious change in any one bracket might have great repercussions by stimulating unforeseen demands from other groups of worker for changes in their wage bracket. In order to minimize these difficulties, the agreement on procedures for establishing wage brackets included a section that read as follows:

> Proposals for changes to wage brackets and job categories shall be drawn up by the Manager responsible after discussions with the Works Committee. Such discussions do not preclude separate sections of the London Factories, or the individual trade unions, from negotiating directly with the Manager responsible in initiating such proposals. It is to be noted, however, that where one trade union is seeking a change, it is desirable that other trade unions shall decide also whether they wish to seek a change, so

that as far as possible these demands will be coordinated in the Works Committee and be pursued concurrently.

II

Discussion with the Works Committee members revealed that they were all sorely pressed over the difficulty of helping the hourly-rated members whom they represented on appeals about merit increases. Merit reviews were carried out once every three months. Each operator was individually reviewed by his manager, and increases in wages were granted or not according to the assessment of the member's work during the preceding period. Failure to receive a merit increase was often the source of much heartburning, and led to appeals on rates in which the shop stewards had to represent the case of the operator.

One striking feature was that although Works Committee members talked about 'the rate for the job', and thought that they worked within a frame of reference of arguing a rate for the job, the true fact was that they did not discuss the rate for the job at all. Although they might describe the work done, they could not measure it, and hence could not relate it to a wage level. Unwittingly, they would therefore use as a basis for discussion the rate for the individual. That is to say, appeals were made on the grounds that the operator himself was worth an increase in pay. As soon as the matter was stated in this way, however, it led to discussion between the operator, the manager, and the shop steward about the personal merits or shortcomings of the operator. All three of them might get drawn into making comparisons between the operator and other members of the department, and possible differences in opinion might arise between the operator and the manager as to the value of the operator himself. Any operator thus appealing was placed in an invidious position —that of having to state his own virtues in arguing for a merit increase.

The situation was further confused by the fact that there was no clear distinction in these discussions on pay between two different, distinct, and important types of grievance: demands for increased pay for the work that the operator was actually doing; and demands for increased pay that were really the reflection of a desire for the opportunity to be given higher levels of work to do, and would in turn call for a higher rate of pay. In other words, discussions on rates were a mixture of argument for more money for work already done, and argument for more responsibility, which would eventually bring higher earnings—a state of affairs that is extremely common in industry generally.

This combination of factors—the failure to discriminate between demands for higher pay for work and demands for higher responsibility, and the posing of rate reviews in terms of the value of the individual rather than in terms of the work he did—tended to make these discussions on wages confused and unsatisfactory. From the point of view of the operator, it was often considered that he had been more than thoroughly discussed, and, whatever the outcome of the discussion, there was always an unsatisfactory feeling left afterwards.

III

To overcome these difficulties, the hourly-rated members were seeking a yardstick for measuring level of work. They had always wanted to be in a position to discuss wages in relation to level of work rather than to the personality and skills of the individual doing the work. If only they had a yardstick, they said, that would enable them to talk about level of work in a measurable way, they could get away from these invidious discussions about individuals and their capacities. The problem, however, was to discover such a yardstick. That was why they had become interested in the developments that had occurred in analysing the work of staff members.

If they had a yardstick it would also solve another problem —that of differentials not as between individuals, but as between different groups and grades of operator. The wage brackets that they had were satisfactory, as far as they went. They did not answer in principle, however, the question of the relative brackets between groups of workers; how, for example, could the wage levels of machinists be settled relative to those of inspectors or storemen? These comparisons of differentials were always lurking in the background as a potential source of stress—stress that might grow slowly and imperceptibly, being experienced as gradually increasing dissatisfaction among given grades of operator with their earnings. Thus, for instance, some machinists engaged in drilling considered that the wage brackets deemed appropriate for their work had become outmoded. Although they could not measure it, they were convinced that they were carrying greater responsibility than they had two or three years before, because of an increase in the amount of heavy duty work that was coming into the factory. This heavy duty work, they maintained, carried a greater responsibility, although they could not state exactly why. One of the criteria they turned to was that heavy duty work was far more difficult to handle. But they realized that if mere physical weight of work was taken as a criterion, it would not lead necessarily to a satisfactory wage structure. Similar mild dissatisfaction, which often threatened to reach more serious proportions, could be found in other groups of hourly-rated members.

IV

Exploratory discussions were arranged, to be held individually with each member of the Works Committee. The goal of these discussions was to find whether there were any characteristics of the work they did that were considered to contain the main elements of responsibility. Because of its usefulness in discussing non-manual jobs, time-span measurement was one of the lines followed. The time-span of discretion was found to be applicable in the hourly-rated jobs that carried responsibility of more than a few days. In shorter-term jobs, however, there did not appear to be such a complete correspondence between time-span, felt responsibility, and the wages considered to be fair. It may be that more accurate measurement and more precise organization will in due course change this picture. In these initial stages of the analysis, however, it appeared to be necessary to elaborate the measuring instrument to distinguish between manual jobs with time-spans of hours, or, at most, of a day or two. The means for just such an elaboration was found by taking into account the factor of avoiding damage to equipment and the scrapping of work. 'Scrap' in this factory is a term used to refer to unsatisfactory work, that is, work rejected on inspection as not up to standard. The importance attached to scrap made it evident that these workers felt pretty sharply their responsibility for turning out satisfactory work. Too high a proportion of scrap led to severe admonition from their manager, possible loss of wages, and, in extreme cases, even to suspension or dismissal.

Following up this lead about scrap, it was decided to examine various jobs to see whether it was possible to discover how much potential scrap could be caused as a result of inadequate discretion on the part of the hourly-rated member. The notion was that the amount of damage that the Company relied on the operator's discretion to avoid might give a measure of the responsibility carried.

This notion of measuring damage-avoidance first posed the question whether the discretionary content of manual work could be distinguished from the prescribed content. The making of such a distinction proved to be quite straightforward for the operators. Although unfamiliar with the idea at first, they soon got down to it and were able to state quite positively that this or that operation required in doing the job called for the use of discretion, whereas other operations were prescribed. Simple operations were described, for example, in which the operator had to put a bearing in a semicircular cup, the cup having an automatic stop and locator so that the bearing could fit only in the correct position. Bringing the tool in contact with the bearing was then a matter either of pushing a button or a lever or pulling a handle. The operation itself was controlled by jigs and fixtures regulated in the initial setting, so that anything that went wrong would be due only to faulty setting or tools and not to bad discretion on the part of the operator. When the operation was finished, it was the operator's job to remove the bearing from the cup and to repeat the operation for the next bearing. One possible reason for scrapping the job would be that swarf had been left in the cup after an operation, but this was not left to discretion. It was prescribed that the cup should be cleaned before each new bearing was put in for machining, and seeing that it was clean required no judgment. The discretionary content of such a job, therefore, was to be found exclusively in the pace at which the operator worked. He was given a standard against which to work, and it required his judgment to keep going at the pace required to turn out the number of bearings called for. The cost of inadequate discretion on such a job would be that of the time lost should the operator use poor discretion and fall behind. The use of poor discretion in this way might be noticed perhaps within half an hour to an hour by the supervisor, who would perceive that the job was not being got ready for the next operation at a sufficient rate.

At the other extreme, there were very complicated jobs like those carried out by highly skilled machinists in setting the machine. A great deal of discretion was required in setting; for example, the grinding of tools by hand called for discretionary control by the operator to get his tool ground just right. Discretion might then be required as to the best way of organizing the work, marking off the job, in the manipulation of tools in such a way as to take cuts of just the right amount to avoid breakage of tooling or marring of work, and judging whether the quality of finish was satisfactory when the work was completed. Jobs of this kind were found in which the operators might be required to work on a particular job, or a batch of work, for periods of two to three weeks, without a full review of their work by their managers.

V

When the potential costs involved in the maximum amount of damage to tools and scrapping of work, as well as maximum potential cost in loss of time, were calculated, it was found that these losses—due solely to bad discretion and not to negligence or mistakes—could range anywhere from a few shillings up to many hundreds of pounds. It became apparent, further, that the jobs that carried the greater amounts of potential discretionary damage in them were the ones that the operators concerned considered should carry higher rates of pay. There thus emerged a possible correlation between the degree of responsibility carried (or level of work done) and the amount of damage-avoidance, that is to say, the amount of wastage the operator was relied upon to avoid through the use of his discretion.

Application of this damage-avoidance concept, it will be seen, depended on the fact that operators were able to discriminate between the discretionary and the prescribed content of their jobs. It must be noted that carrying out the discretionary elements of a manual job differed in certain respects, however, from carrying out the discretionary elements of a non-manual job. Its particular characteristic was that it called for perceptual or sensory judgment by the person doing the job. It was the kind of judgment or discrimination usually referred to as skill—or as having a feel for the job, or the knack of doing it. When judgment or discretion was removed from a job by the design and prescribed use of special jigs, tools, and fixtures, the level of work was experienced as decreasing, and the job described as being de-skilled.

The level of work in a job depended on the extent to which doing the job as prescribed called for discretion by the operator. This meant that level of work could not be related in a general way to any particular kind of operation being done. It could not be maintained, for example, that drilling, say, required a higher level of work than milling or grinding. It depended on the actual job being done. Thus, a single-spindle drill might be used for relatively low levels of work if the particular job that was being carried out had standardized jigs, tools, and fixtures. If, on the other hand, the particular job had not been tooled up in this way, and more discretion and judgment were required of the operator doing the job, then work on the self-same machine might well be at a much higher level.

Another instance of different levels of work being carried out on the same machine was that of the automatic machines. These are hopper-fed machines that carry on at a fixed pace. They may be operated at the level of work involved in hopper-feeding, and in knowing enough to turn the machine off when it sounds as though there is some trouble—a supervisor coming by every fifteen minutes or so to see that everything is running smoothly. Or they may be operated at the level of work required in keeping the machine running—setting it, getting over blockages and breakdowns, and re-setting when required, so that the machine keeps going from hour to hour throughout the day without any need for supervision. To ascertain the different levels of work possible for running the same machine, the actual discretion left to the operator had to be worked out in each individual and specific instance.

VI

In view of these early results, the Works Committee decided to duplicate the procedure used originally by the staff committees in carrying out a preliminary test of the time-span notion. They arranged for discussions about their work with a number of hourly-rated operators engaged in a wide variety of jobs. Each of these operators asked his supervisor or section manager whether he would also participate in the study, giving an independent analysis of the operator's job. These discussions were carried through with the following results, reported by the Works Committee to the Works Council in June 1955:

(a) all the operators found it possible to distinguish the discretionary aspects of their jobs from the prescribed or routine aspects;

(b) all the supervisors or section managers found it equally possible to distinguish the discretionary content of the jobs of operators subordinate to them;

(c) there was consistency in all instances where there were independent assessments of the same operator's job by himself and by his supervisor or section manager;

(d) it was possible in most cases to estimate the maximum potential loss; and the evidence—although tentative—suggested that there was a connection between the amount of potential damage and what an operator and his superior or manager would consider a fair rate within given general wage levels.

These initial results suggested an underlying hourly-rated wage structure dependent upon the amount of wastage that the operator was expected to use his discretion to avoid. This avoidance of wastage was not familiar to the operator who knew his job. When he was doing his job, if he was paid satisfactorily for it, he used his judgment or discretion without being aware of it. In the case of a new operator in training, however, the discretionary components of the job were very readily observable. They were those elements that the operator found awkward to perform. It might take him some time to acquire the so-called skill and experience to be able to make the necessary judgment with ease and comfort, and to be able to forget he was doing so.

One further finding of some interest must be mentioned. In those instances where it was possible to make comparisons between hourly-rated and staff jobs of the same maximum time-span (that is to say, jobs with maximum time-spans over three or four days), the hourly-rated members and the staff members, in discussing what they considered to be a fair return for their own jobs, mentioned wage and salary levels that were very similar. This observed connection was very suggestive of the more general conclusion that the time-span itself was an indirect measure of the amount of resources under the discretionary control of the member carrying out any job. It was further suggestive of the notion that wage and salary structures were thrown up in relation to the maximum quantity of the firm's resources—time, equipment, materials, work of other members—that it put under the discretionary control of each member, thus entrusting him with the responsibility for avoiding waste or loss of those resources.

CHAPTER VI

The Current Situation

I

UNDER the conditions of work with the Company, the full details of the work done are not generally available. Only in some instances have conditions allowed for the publication of the details of specific jobs. This situation is gradually changing as analysis of more and more jobs is worked through as between manager and subordinates. Even so, however, it still remains for the Company to discover for itself whether or not the instruments described have practical value and are usable in a ready way by themselves. The current situation is that just such an exploration has been commenced within the firm's executive system, and some results have already been obtained. This exploration was initiated by a report from the social-analyst to the Works Council in March 1955. The report summarized and pulled together for the first time the main points that had emerged from the analysis.

The report pointed out that the members of the firm were —without being aware of it—operating a systematic set of principles governing status and grading. Because they were unaware of these principles, they had difficulty in implementing them with consistency, and hence trouble arose.

These unrecognized principles were threefold. First, status

and payment were accorded for the level of work that a person was expected to do and succeeded in doing, and not for his skill, experience, training, or qualifications. Second, the level of work allocated to a person could be defined solely in terms of the decisions that he was called upon to take and act upon in his job, and except in these terms was not related to the quality of the results achieved nor to those aspects of method that were prescribed. Third, what they experienced as level of work was the span of time during which a member was authorized to make his own decisions without opportunity of reference to his manager for judgment of their quality or a decision to change or to re-affirm his terms of reference; and in the case of manual work, the direct calculation of the amount of damage that might be caused if inadequate discretion were exercised.

The report went on to point out that the analysis in no way implied that a person's skill and experience were unimportant; on the contrary, skill and experience were what determined the level of work he might receive, and thus, at second hand, his status and pay. Usually skill and experience and level of work were consistent with each other. When, however, a person's skill or experience were greater than the level of work he did, then he got paid for his work and not his experience. Moreover, status and payment appeared to be given for what might seem to be negative reasons—that is to say, they were given for the amount of damage or loss to Company resources (including time) that a member was expected to avoid in doing his work, i.e. in making the decisions required of him.

If these propositions turned out to be correct, and were implemented as policy, discussion of salaries or wages would become a matter of objective assessment of the level of work that a manager gave his subordinates to do, and would not be concerned with the personal characteristics or abilities of the subordinate himself. The subordinate would be entitled to expect pay and status in line with the maximum level of work he was expected to discharge. Objectively to measure level of work and hence to assess status and salary or wage would get rid of some of the argument currently engaged in.

There would, however, remain room for argument about the level of work a member should be allocated by his manager. The granting of opportunity for work of increasing scope or difficulty raised the question of a manager's judgment of the skill and trustworthiness of his subordinates. In the final analysis, there arose the question of selection and promotion of members to responsibilities at higher levels—and consequently carrying higher status and pay.

Discussions between managers and subordinates became confused just as soon as questions of fair salary were mixed up with questions of individual capacity and opportunity for advancement. If salary and opportunity were discussed at the same time, there was a fair chance that neither of the issues would get discussed effectively. If, however, these questions were dealt with separately, there was a good chance of settling the issue of fair remuneration for level of work done. This issue being settled, managers and subordinates could get closer to grips with the whole question of careers and opportunities for advancement for individuals, without the confusing element of payment for work currently done constantly dogging the discussion.

The report pointed out, in conclusion, that if the analysis presented was correct, it meant that the Company would have to decide whether to try to effect a very considerable reorientation towards the whole question of work, status, and salaries. This reorientation required a change to the use of level of work as the fundamental consideration in resolving problems of status, salaries, and wages.

The required reorientation might prove more difficult for members in higher executive positions. The higher one's position, the more difficult it was to understand it, in the sense of the ability to appreciate it in terms of an analysis of one's own job. Shorter time-span jobs tended to consist of only a single task. When each task was completed the next was taken up. Time-span was relatively easily calculated under these conditions. The longest time-span jobs, however, tended to contain many tasks at the same time. Calculating the overall time-span was likely, therefore, to be a more complex matter.

II

The Works Council, in considering the report, concluded that exploration had gone sufficiently far by that time for them to begin to assess these notions for themselves. With the strong support of the Managing Director (who, it may be recalled, was one of the Council members), it was decided that an exploration would be carried out within the executive system to discover the consequence of measuring the Company's jobs in terms of time-span. This analysis would be carried out by the firm's Policy Research Officer[1] on behalf of the Managing Director, who would in due course report the results to the Works Council.

Preliminary results have shown that it is possible for an executive member of the Company itself to analyse jobs in the Company in terms of time-span. The Managing Director's report to the Works Council in July 1955 contained the following:

> I have received up to now two written reports from the Policy Research Officer concerning the preliminary results arising from executive work on this matter. In the three months following the last report to Council (at the end of March), some 150 hours of discussion have taken place with members, and a great deal of material has been

[1] The title of the firm's member who is executively in charge of research and development work in the social and organizational field.

collected concerning some 50 roles. Much more time has been spent on sifting and categorizing this material, and this process is still going on concurrently with the collection of further data.

Two things emerge from the investigation so far as it has gone at the moment. First, so far as the preliminary results go, they tend to confirm the findings of the social-analyst. Secondly, the members concerned have found this means of assessing work to be valuable. In the light of these experiences, I have discussed preliminary proposals with the Policy Research Officer, which I am hoping to be able to discuss with my subordinates within three months. They will thereafter almost inevitably have to undergo considerable discussion at lower levels of the executive system. Subject to their appearing realistic, I will be able to bring them to Council. In the meantime I hope to bring to Council, so far as possible each month, an account of the stage matters have reached.

This work is being currently pursued by the Policy Research Officer. Managers are being aided in getting out an analysis of all the positions subordinate to them in terms of their discretionary content and time-span. In this way progress is being made towards a specification of the range of level of work in many positions in the firm, and the setting up of a central job specifications record room. The data so collected, it is anticipated, will be used for a variety of purposes, as, for example, analysis of organization, advertising, and selection, and planning future personnel requirements. Furthermore, these data will be used as the basis for discussions on policy governing the Company's wage and salary structure, and its status and grading arrangements. In the course of carrying through this programme, members are being trained in the use of time-span analysis, so that managers can assess their subordinates' work, and subordinates can ensure the accuracy and completeness of these assessments.

III

With respect to publication of salary bracket figures, the Works Council decided at its meeting in July 1955, that the general salary levels with respect to time-span should be publicly reported in the firm. These are the figures presented in Chapter Four. This decision represented a radical change in Company policy. The effects of such publication cannot be reported, as the change has only just taken place. But some notion of the difficulties that the firm has tried to overcome by anticipating them may be derived from the proceedings of the July Council meeting at which this decision was taken. The tenor of the discussion may be of interest to others outside the firm, precisely because of the picture it portrays of some of the real difficulties to be encountered.

The proposal that raised the issue was a report from the Council's Steering Committee, which ran as follows:

> In May last year, Council decided to confirm the terms of reference of the research on status and grading, as previously minuted, notwithstanding the possible implications of the work of the social-analyst as regards implicit disclosure of salary brackets.
>
> Council is now informed that a report from the social-analyst is available, setting out the regular pattern of salaries which his analysis indicates to be currently expected for work as measured by time-span, and the trend in this pattern over the past two years. This report will be presented at the next meeting of Council, should this be Council's wish.

The Managing Director opened the discussion. He said that he understood that this publication would consist in general terms of a list of time-spans—one-day, one-week, one-month, one-year, two-year, and so on—and against each of these periods would be quoted a bracket of pay or salary that had been found to be consistent with the maximum length of time-span. He was anxious about the effect of this publication, in the sense that Council meetings in the last six months had on each occasion given rise to a considerable amount of work for his subordinates. There was clearly a strong possibility that many people might essay the task of calculating their own time-span, and many, in the absence of the required skill, might come to conclusions they believed in and make assessments as to how they stood in relation to a particular bracket. As a result, managers might be faced with a considerable volume of work about salaries. For this reason he was first of all minded to vote against publication, on the grounds that it would be better to delay it until the maximum time-span of at least a large proportion of roles in the Company had been worked out.

But he then thought about what the effect would be of his going to Council and saying that he would not vote for it. This might raise just as much anxiety and argument about salaries and brackets, and he might be faced with a situation where people said, 'We are anxious to get on with assessing what are the appropriate status, grading, and pay for a large number of people on the basis of research that has been done, and you—one of the proponents of this—are the first to object to the official publication of data that will prove valuable'. He did not know which was the correct way to vote on this. He was in a dilemma: if he voted against it, people would say, 'He won't let it be published because he knows we will be able to see we are underpaid'; if he voted in favour, people might make calculations with no validity, at a time when the Company did not want to be involved in arguments until they could properly assess these in terms of the work being done by the Policy Research Officer.

The Grade I representative said that if there was such a report available, it would be advisable for it to be submitted to Council. If the document existed, some garbled account was likely to get round by 'bush telegraph'. In view of the Managing Director's comments, it might be advisable to refer the matter back to constituent bodies, however, and to decide whether or not publication should go ahead.

Grade II said they had not realized the implications for the Managing Director. They had been all in favour of the publication as soon as possible. Investigations had been going on for a number of years, and—although they were already getting somewhere—they felt there should be some really concrete results now. If the Managing Director had any suggestions to make as to how to limit come-back, they would consider them. Would it, for example, be possible to accept the report on condition that no queries were raised on the basis of its content until the Policy Research Officer's results were published?

The Managing Director said that, so long as there was widespread realization of the difficulties that would arise if people unscientifically "worked out" their maximum time-spans and used these inaccurate findings to check their salaries against the published brackets and raise queries and appeals, then he had no objection to the report being published.

The Chairman reminded Council that Management had the Policy Research Officer working on status and grading, and any such anxieties in members could be taken care of by him in his investigations in due course.

The Grade III representative said that quite a large number of staff knew about time-span, but did not know enough to be able to work it out. He would hope that anyone with such queries would go to his representative. He wanted to confirm that if publication was disallowed it would lead to some feeling.

The representative of the Association of Engineering and Shipbuilding Draughtsmen expressed surprise at the discussion. The social-analyst's reports related status and grading to salary. There appeared to be a great deal of consistency between salary and time-span throughout industry. People would move to another job if they thought they did not get the right salary—they knew already whether they were satisfied with their salary. He did not think there was need for any fears that publication of time-spans relative to salary brackets would cause any great worry to Management.

The Managing Director agreed the coincidence between time-span and salaries, but doubted if there was any coincidence between salaries and the time-spans members might work out for themselves in unscientific calculations. He then asked whether the report could be suitably endorsed to the effect that, whether or not individuals felt themselves capable of making their own calculations about time-span, appeals for revisions of salaries on this basis would not be heard until some firm policy had been agreed.

A proposal was adopted that the salary data should be published in September 1955. This proposal, as approved, carried a rider. When put forward, the report should be endorsed by the Steering Committee to the effect that, for sound technical reasons, it was not yet possible for individual members to calculate their own time-spans; there was a coincidence between time-spans and salaries, but it was unlikely that there would be at this stage a coincidence between salaries and the time-spans that might be worked out by members in unscientific calculations.

IV

Finally, the social-analytic work is continuing within the terms of reference set by the Works Council. Questions of selection are being studied in conjunction with both hourly-rated and staff members who have volunteered to review the development of their careers in terms of the maximum level of work they have been capable of performing at various stages. The Company's Standing Orders on procedures for promotion and appointments are being considered in the light of the developments in time-span measurement. And methods are emerging for assessing likely shortages of personnel, and the likely pressures towards promotion or towards labour turnover, by analysis of the age distribution of members occupying various groups of job categorized according to range of level of work. The general direction of the work as a whole is towards a systematic analysis of work organization in terms of the interaction of level of work, individual capacity, payment, job opportunities, and career development.

PART III

Theoretical Considerations

CHAPTER VII

Notes on the Psychological Meaning of Work

I

THE conclusions to be drawn from the events and developments of the past three years may be summarized in one general statement. When level of work is measured by time-span (including where necessary the wastage-avoidance notion), an equitable work-payment structure can be found: payment that is consistent with this structure will be found satisfying by members fully established in jobs; work will be done in a relatively efficient, competitive, and decisive manner within the limits of the form of organization adopted; and there will be freedom from grievances about differentials between members and between groups or grades of members.

The above statement assumes a definition of work as the totality of prescribed and discretionary activities that a person does in discharging the responsibilities he has contracted to undertake in order to earn his living. Moreover, concealed within the statement—in the prescription for measuring level of work—is the notion that what is experienced as one's level of work has only to do with the use of discretion and judgment, and has nothing whatever to do with the prescribed content of one's work. These definitions of work and of level of work have been tacitly used in the preceding part of the book. They can no longer simply be taken for granted. Before proceeding further, we must examine them, discover what their implications might be, and see whether any justification can be found for their use.

II

I have limited my use of the idea of discretion and judgment to discretion and judgment that eventuate in definite and observable actions, in decisions that end in someone doing something—issuing an order, setting a policy, writing a report, machining some metal, making a drawing. I have excluded from this definition any idea of decisions that someone makes in thought, but that do not eventually get expressed in action observable by others. It is executive discretion and judgment that are being considered—the use of discretion and judgment in doing something, which may be preceded by thinking about it, but is not confined to thinking about it.

Discretion and judgment are demanded when there are more ways than one to go about doing a particular job. In executive systems, a person's being confronted with alternatives applies only to parts of any job. Every job is limited in some of its aspects, in the sense that complete freedom to use discretion or judgment is definitely not allowed. When we talk about discretion and judgment, therefore, we are talking about those aspects of a job in which the person is *allowed* to choose, and indeed *required* to choose, from among alternative ways of doing something, as opposed to those aspects in which he is *prohibited* from choosing and must follow a prescribed policy or method. In non-manual work this process of choice is usually experienced and described as deciding, or making and acting upon decisions; in manual work it is experienced as judging, or getting the feel of, or guessing just the right way to do a task—just how much more pressure is needed in drilling something, just what tool angle should be used for cutting, or just when a process has reached the right colour and appearance.

The prescribed and the discretionary components of a job interact in the following way. The prescribed elements constitute a boundary around a job. They set limits to what the person in the job may do. They state what he may not do. They also state the things he must do—the regulations, the policies, the methods, the routines, to which he must conform. Within these limits the person must use discretion. He must use his own judgment. He must choose what he thinks is the best course when faced with alternative possibilities. He must seek alternative possibilities. From this point of view, being able to set precise limits to a job is a positive and constructive action of immense importance. It frees a subordinate to concentrate his use of discretion within his own field of operation. It limits uncertainty within manageable bounds.

Realistic regulations, routines, and procedures may thus have a liberating rather than a constricting effect on initiative and the use of discretion. Failure to have clear limits established for him bogs a person down in problems that are not germane to his immediate job, and this causes inefficiency. The advantages of setting firm and stated limits in this way are commonly subscribed to in the notion that it is important for members to know where they stand. If we now turn our attention exclusively to the problem of discretion and judgment, it may be appreciated that this is not to minimize the importance of the prescribed content of work. It is merely to state that prescribed content is not relevant to our present considerations of payment and status.

An important feature in discretion and judgment, and a feature that may lead immediately to the heart of our problem, has to do with the nature of choice. When someone is faced with a decision, he is faced not only with the problem of choosing which is the best course of action, and then of following that course. He is also faced with the opposite problem.

He must decide against the other courses open to him; he must give up these courses; he must put them aside. Everyone must be familiar with the experience of arriving at a difficult decision and having, because of circumstances, to act upon it, although still not sure whether or not it was the wisest course to take. How desirable some of the rejected courses often become in retrospect, while one is waiting to discover from the results whether the course chosen will turn out to have been a good one! Gnawing doubts and uncertainties of this kind give rise to much of the worry that attends difficult work.

A further complication must now be added. Executive work does not consist of one decision and the job is done. It consists of a continuous series of decisions. No sooner is one choice made, and the consequent path negotiated, than the next corner is reached, and another choice is required. Some paths lead up blind alleys; other paths lead to the final objective, but are more difficult or take longer; and some paths lead through expeditiously. Only when the task is completed is it possible to get it into perspective—sometimes clearly, sometimes only vaguely—and discover which choices, if any, might have made it easier. Furthermore, in jobs at higher time-span levels (commonly in all jobs over several months' time-span) there is more than one task to be done at a time. That is to say, there is more than one series of decisions to be negotiated —some long, some short, and none of them in phase with each other. Decisions with respect to entirely different tasks have to be made in succession.

Reinforcing the doubts that may be stimulated in decision-making is the uncertainty, always present, that arises because better alternatives may remain unrecognized and unknown. There are always better alternatives that have not been thought of. Decision-making calls for a fine balance to be held between, on the one hand, choosing right away from among the best alternatives available so as to do what needs to be done at the time, and on the other hand seeking, trying out, and bringing into play at the appropriate moment new means for doing the same job in a more effective way. This fine balance is exercised by everybody in every job—manual and non-manual, managerial and non-managerial—most often intuitively and without thinking about it. Sometimes, usually at higher levels in organizations, intuitive exercise of the balance is reinforced by setting up special development and research jobs or departments.

When a person is well settled in a job that is 'just right for him', he ordinarily does not experience doubt and vacillation and indecisiveness. His job carries a challenge to judgment and discretion. But the challenge is of such a kind that he can at least detect differences between the courses of action from which he must choose only one and commit himself to it. A too easy job is one in which the best course of those available is so self-evident as to require no effort of choice. A too difficult job is one that presents courses of action between which the individual is simply unable to perceive any difference: all the courses appear equally attractive or unattractive, equally sensible or impossible; and choosing and deciding become a matter of gambling, or tossing a coin, with the sense of despair that goes along with such a position if one's job hangs in the balance.

III

Since decision-making as we have described it involves the giving up of those courses of action that have been rejected, the capacity to tolerate uncertainty will be seen to play a considerable part in the capacity to do work. Tolerance of uncertainty, and the giving up of alternative choices in order to choose a particular path to a goal, are characteristics of personality that can be seen to grow and develop in the individual. In the very early days of infancy, immediate gratification of needs is required if frustration is to be forestalled.

As tolerance grows, a greater capacity develops to put off desirable events or pleasures with the promise, if delay is accepted, of getting something better. The capacity to choose a delayed course of action, rather than immediate gratification, is one that does not ordinarily develop until after the second or third year, and may not appear until much later, even in rudimentary form.[1] For to choose a delayed course means to be able to weigh the chances for or against a greater return if delay is accepted. Couched in these terms, our illustration may be seen to be a description of an early and primitive form of investment behaviour—a prototype of later patterns of investment decision. The gratifying prospects of success are weighed against the anxiety or worry attendant upon the possibility of loss in the event of failure, or, more simply, against the frustration and loss of liquidity or immediate gratification arising merely from waiting, even in conditions of relative certainty.

As the individual grows and develops, he becomes capable of tolerating for increasingly long periods of time the uncertainty arising out of committing himself to a course of decisions. There is no reason to believe that this capacity develops to the same degree in everyone. Individuals vary considerably in what we may term their time-span capacity; that is to say, the length of time for which they are able to tolerate the effects of exercising discretion on their own account in pursuit of a living. It is likely that intellectual ability sets limits to time-span capacity, but is not itself the sole factor of importance. Low intelligence precludes high time-span; but high intelligence does not necessarily mean high time-span capacity,

---

[1] Melanie Klein has frequently pointed out that the duration of gratifying or frustrating experiences in early infancy has a profound effect on later development. (Cf, for example, her paper 'A Study of Envy and Gratitude', delivered to the International Psycho-Analytic Congress in 1955.) The infant's reactions to these early experiences, in particular those having to do with the periods in between feeding, and the absences of his mother, establish a rigid foundation upon which there later grows the capacity to tolerate uncertainty for greater or lesser periods of time.

any more than high intelligence automatically leads to vocational success. If our analysis is correct, emotional make-up as well as intelligence must enter in view of the importance of the factor of being able to tolerate uncertainty. To take an extreme example, high intelligence does not in itself compensate in work for emotional instability and impulsiveness. In the short term, good results may be achieved, but impulsiveness and instability will weigh against a person's capacity to discharge responsibility over any extended period of time without review.

IV

The capacity to exercise discretion for longer or shorter periods of time is an outcome of the capacity to anticipate the sequence of events that will follow from any particular action. This anticipation may be conscious, or intuitive, or a mixture of conscious imagination and intuition. Perception will, of course, become more cloudy the farther into the future the chain of events is traced in one's mind. It may be that the length of time into the future that likely consequences can be traced is related to the capacity mentally to organize previous experience.[1] One possibility that suggests itself is that a person's time-span is that period of time over which he can look back and perceive in an organized way a continuous sequence of events leading up to circumstances in his current work situation.

[1] At deeper levels psychologically, this capacity to organize previous experience is connected with the quality and intensity of unconscious anxiety, in particular of what is termed paranoid anxiety. In her paper, 'The Importance of Symbol Formation in the Development of the Ego', (in *Contributions to Psycho-Analysis*, London: 1948), Melanie Klein has shown the relationship between severe inhibitions in learning and the inability to deal with extremes of unconscious infantile sadistic impulses. It is these extremes of sadism in very early infancy that give rise to the deep-seated paranoid anxieties, which have a profoundly inhibiting effect on learning and upon all work in general. Anxieties of this kind militate against the ability to use past experience, and hence will diminish time-span capacity. In severely disturbed individuals, the capacity to do work is reduced practically to zero.

Thus, as we get to the higher and higher time-spans, we may be dealing with greater capacity to utilize longer and longer stretches of past experience. Statesmanship illustrates the point. A statesman must be of historical bent, and requires to have (apart from other historical knowledge) the past fifty or one hundred years of a nation's history available in a living way within himself to be brought to bear upon making decisions of state. By way of contrast, academic historians and archaeologists are not necessarily in possession of time-span capacity equivalent to the number of years that the period they are studying occupies in the past. We are concerned with the capacity to organize past experience as connected with the present in a continuous sequence. The work of the historian and archaeologist is in this particular respect usually directed towards the unconnected past. Their time-spans would be measured by the discretion and judgment they use currently in the present, in planning, organizing, and carrying out historical or archaeological studies of the past.

V

From the point of view put forward, work may be described as a kind of investment behaviour—investment in one's foresight, one's ability to foresee the consequences of one's actions. The bigger the job the bigger the problem of investment, in the sense that the longer is the series of decisions to be negotiated and the longer the periods of foresight required. *So also, the longer is the period of uncertainty about the wisdom of the investments being made.* For an employed person, the investment is of a special kind. He is authorized to invest the resources of his employer in his own foresight for the time-span governing the job.

Work in the above sense of investment and foresight may be contrasted with scientific prediction and gambling, in both of which a sequence of happenings is predicted with a known degree of certainty. The probability of a given result, or the odds on any particular outcome, can always be stated. Executive work contains some scientific knowledge and prediction, and some elements of gambling. But it is different from either of them in a very important respect. Its central feature is the mental working out of the various alternative paths, and the choice of what seems the best, without the benefit of any knowledge whatever about the probability or degree of certainty of a given result occurring. This mental working-through is mainly unconscious; it takes place automatically most of the time, and only makes itself felt when a person finds himself faced by a difficult problem.[1]

We may thus carry our psychological definition of work one step further. What is experienced as size of job, or level of work, is the experience of the passing of time during which a series of decisions is made and a sequence of actions carried out without the individual's being able to know until some time later how good has been the discretion and judgment applied. The size of a job is the maximum period of time demanded by the conditions of the job with respect to one's being able to tolerate making fresh decisions in the face of continuing uncertainty. Weight of responsibility has been translated into time of responsibility. Being weighed down by too much responsibility means, in these terms, being exposed to continuous uncertainty for such long periods as to induce insecurity, lack of sureness, and anxiety.

VI

An important question now poses itself. Is it to be construed that an individual has a given capacity at any given

[1] This notion of work is made explicit in the Latin use of *labor* and *opus*. *Labor* is the work or toil that precedes and accompanies the carrying out of the task or *opus*. *Labor* is often used in the sense of the toil or effort that must go on inside oneself in order to set to the task. It is recognized as an emotionally trying process. *Hoc opus, hic labor est.* The ability to toil underlies true knowledge and wisdom—to both of which are often attributed pain and tribulation, an attribution that is due largely to the content of emotional toil.

stage in his development to undertake work of a particular maximum span of time? Findings on this subject, though limited in scope and number, are consistent, and do suggest such a construction; although, just as with other characteristics of personality make-up, a person's time-span capacity at any given time need not be taken as absolutely fixed and incapable of change.[1] If we pursue the implications of such a construction sufficiently far, we may discover that it will help us to explain certain otherwise puzzling matters, although our explanations may not always be in accord with established or traditional views.

Explorations of their work history with individuals employed at Glacier and elsewhere suggest a regular pattern in the development of the time-span capacity of each individual. Examples of what were deemed by the individuals

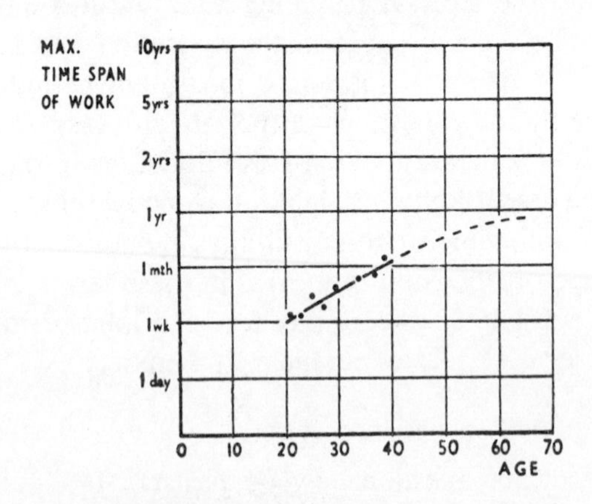

[1] We have already indicated in a previous section that time-span capacity is a compound of intelligence and emotional make-up. As such it would be modifiable under the same conditions as other deep-rooted personal characteristics like stability or temperament. Ordinary educational or training procedures would be expected to have little, if any, effect in bringing about consciously planned attempts at individual development. It is likely that more intensive procedures would be required, aimed at deep-rooted personality change, of the kind to be achieved with full-scale individual psycho-analysis.

to be the biggest jobs they had done at various stages in their careers were analysed in terms of the maximum time-span of discretion carried. When these maximum time-spans were plotted on a graph with respect to age, a regular progression could be found, as illustrated in the adjoining curve.

When the findings from a number of individual analyses of the above kind are put together, curves of the following

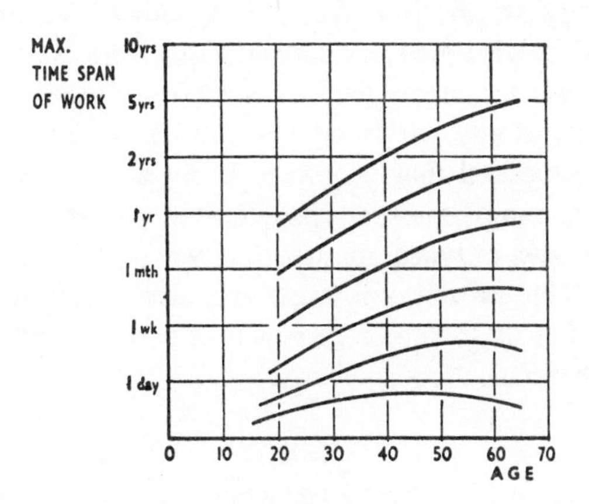

general shape are suggested. Time-span capacity gradually increases until middle life, at which time the increase slows or stops. At the lower time-span levels, the process of increase probably stops in the early thirties, and there may be some subsequent recession. The tailing-off process appears to occur towards the mid-forties at higher time-span levels. At the very high levels, time-span capacity may increase throughout life.[1]

The pattern of the curves suggests the need for two conceptions: that of the *current time-span capacity* of an individual—his time-span capacity at his current age; and the

[1] The curves appear to be of the type of normal growth and decay processes, the full train of which is not encompassed within the normal span of life. The peak of the process is reached in the early thirties at the lower time-span levels, and very late in life, or not at all, in the very high time-span range. Hence, more of the phase of diminution or decrease in capacity is seen in the lower time-span range.

potential time-span capacity of an individual—his maximum likely time-span capacity in the future. The above curve is that of a person with a current time-span capacity of about six months, and a potential time-span capacity of something over one year.

It has not escaped our attention that the work from which this family of curves has been derived is based upon a very far-reaching assumption. We have assumed that any given individual has a time-span capacity that will exert a strong force in determining the level of work he will seek and carry successfully at any particular point in his career. Moreover, we have supposed that people seek out careers in terms of their developing time-spans, so that in maturity they may achieve a level of work adapted to their potential time-span capacity. This assumption must be critically scrutinized and assessed. Let us therefore elaborate it further, and examine it in more detail.

VII

Our thesis is this. Individuals who work full-time, and who elect to work in industry, will press towards finding work at a level corresponding to their current time-span capacity. We have carefully limited our thesis to work in industry; and to persons who are dependent for their living on full-time work. How far this thesis might apply outside these limits will not be considered. It is too big a question. It would extend, for instance, to the question of persons whose work is a vocation, and who are held to accept work at lower levels than they are capable of managing, because of the satisfaction of a personal or ethical kind to be derived from the particular content of the responsibility. It would also extend to artists and others engaged in creative work, or to persons in individual professional work. These areas of work must remain outside the present analysis. The data are not available for considering them.

The meaning of the above thesis can be described as follows. A person in a job that is consistent with his current time-span capacity and that allows for the taking on of added responsibility as his current time-span capacity increases with age will experience a sense of well-being so far as the work content of his job is concerned. And he will not be experienced by his manager as either pushing or slacking. If his work is at a level higher or lower than his current time-span capacity, he will take steps to gain work at his own level—either by pressing on through special effort to get increasing responsibilities, or else by arranging matters so as to off-load responsibility on to his manager or on to his colleagues. The farther his job is from a level of work corresponding to his current time-span capacity, the greater will be the effort he will put into gaining work at his own level. A person who has been actively pushing to change his level of work will reduce his efforts to do so as he approaches work at his current time-span capacity. He will go on pushing only if he is frustrated in his efforts to gain his correct level of work.

In the foregoing, due emphasis must be placed upon the fact that we have formulated our propositions in terms of an individual *seeking* a level of work consistent with his current time-span capacity. These propositions *do not* mean that every individual finds his correct level of work all the time; nor do they mean that an individual's time-span level is fixed and immutable. It is readily apparent, for example, that in times of depression, or of rapid change in industrial organization, or of shifting of population, individuals become dislocated to a greater or lesser degree, and are likely to find themselves depressed in level of work. Under such conditions, our thesis would state, each individual will exert strenuous effort to regain his proper level of work. If there are too strong barriers counteracting these efforts operating against too many people at any one time, as in times of economic depression, the dammed-up pressures towards higher levels of work will contribute significantly to the explosiveness of the situation that may arise.

What we mean when we say a person will press for work at his own current time-span capacity may be illustrated in the following three examples.

1. In the accompanying diagram, let AC represent the

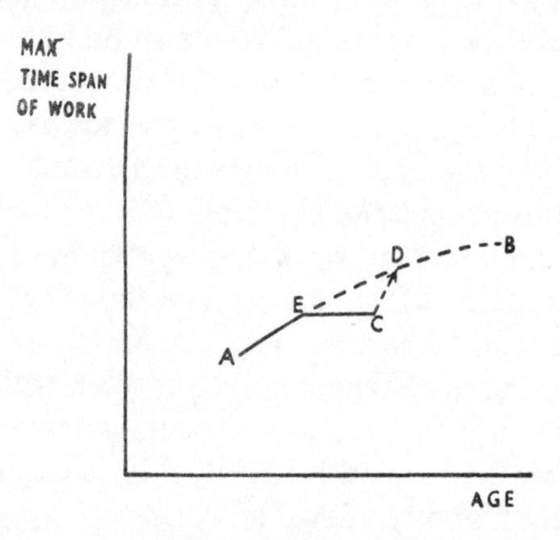

actual course of the development of a particular individual in his career in terms of maximum time-span of work achieved. Our thesis would lead us to expect that circumstances at E had frustrated his normal advancement. We would predict that he would begin to exert increasing pressure to get ahead. He would continue to exert this pressure until he regained his appropriate level of work at, say, point D. At this stage, the additional pressure would drop off, and he would proceed along his normal course of advancement towards B. Occasion to study their circumstances with individuals who could be described as being in such a position has shown that they exert these additional pressures by such means as: seeking and getting a change in job within the same firm; seeking a new job elsewhere; applying for a managerial traineeship; deciding to undertake first training and then work in an entirely new field, even where this might mean an initial drop in status and income.

2. If an individual with a time-span curve was working in a job whose range of level of work was XY, the following

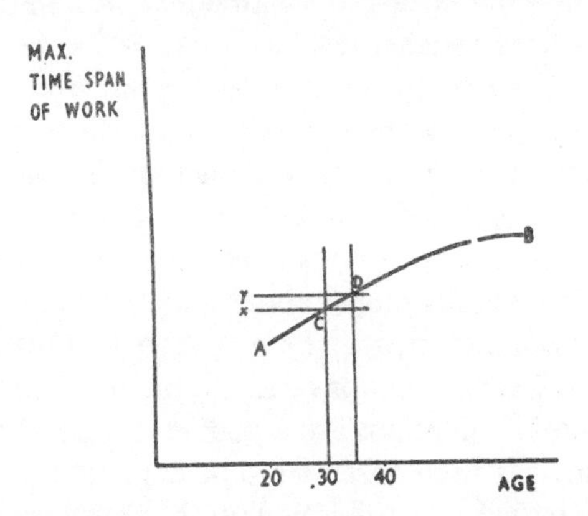

predictions would be made. He would not have been appointed to the job in the first place until he was approaching the age of 30. He would begin to become dissatisfied with the work available to him—finding it too easy or too dull—if he was still in the job as he approached the age of 35. Our own experience is in accord with these predictions. We have become familiar with persons in such circumstances beginning to think again about their careers and futures, as they approached the upper limits of current jobs, and contemplating a change to another job with more scope, or else seeking promotion.

3. Another type of situation, whose occurrence is not unfamiliar, is that of the person who feels his job grow out from under him. The level of work in his job may be reduced by standardization or by other change in method or work content. Or its level of work may be increased as a result of organizational expansion of new types of work calling for a higher level of discretion and responsibility. Changes of this

kind are constantly occurring to a greater or lesser degree in the flux and flow of market conditions and new technology. Such circumstances could be predicted to have the following characteristics.

If level of work drops, the individual will start to exert pressure towards a higher level of work, or else he will resist the changes in method that are reducing the level of work in the job he occupies. When it is resistance to change that takes place, the resistance usually manifests itself in terms of arguments about wages and salaries, rather than about changes in work. In the absence of objective measures of work level, money is more readily talked about than the work that gives rise to it. In our experience, the managers and the members concerned with such situations end up equally frustrated, even though makeshift solutions are found. A much more satisfactory outcome has been observed to be experienced when the justification or lack of justification for the change in work content has been argued out and resolved; and when, in addition, principles have been agreed for changes in jobs for the individuals whose current jobs suffer reduction in level of work.

When an increase in level of work occurs in jobs, the effects will be different from those following a drop in level. If the increase in level is not too much in advance of a person's own rate of increase in current time-span capacity, then he may succeed in adjusting. If, however, the rate of increase in level of work is too rapid, the mental and emotional strain upon the individual may become intolerable—showing up in the form of what is commonly experienced in industry as difficulty in coping, evading responsibility, over-burdening of subordinates, failure to plan ahead, and, as a final outcome, even reaching the stage of personal illness.

VIII

The above thesis and the three illustrations raise a very important question. Is it considered that no persons fully employed in industry in order to earn their living ever permanently accept work of shorter time-span than is warranted by their current time-span capacity? It is commonly argued that precisely such an abnegation of advancement often enough occurs in our society. The motives described for such behaviour are various. Some individuals are reputed to set aside advancement in order not to have to part from their working group. Others are said to avoid too great responsibility at work, in order to pursue hobbies, or avocations, or voluntary services of benefit to the community. The lesser responsibility at work is supposedly compensated for by the greater emotional satisfaction derived from the activities outside work. The thesis outlined would suggest that these commonly held notions ought not to be accepted at their face value. A further critical examination may be warranted.

Re-examination of the following experiences in the light of the above thesis tended to support the notion that the commonly held view of these matters may well be in not very close accord with reality. One has had the opportunity on a number of occasions to note persons who had renounced higher levels of work that they were reputedly capable of doing, and who had subsequently been persuaded, for whatever reason, to accept promotion to the higher levels. On such occasions, the reactions of the persons concerned have been characteristic and consistent. One might have expected a more or less grudging acceptance of the new responsibilities, with indications that the work could be done if the person chose to do it. But such was not the case. The common reaction was breakdown in the face of the new responsibilities. A person who was good at his previous job had been lost for one who was a failure at the higher level. Such evidence, it is recognized, is very far indeed from the sort of evidence that would allow any definite conclusions to be drawn. But it has been found to be very difficult to discover instances that support the commonly held view and that can bear detailed scrutiny.

This question that we have raised will have to be left open. The material presented, however, does allow the issue to be formulated in a manner that can be examined. It is suggested that patterns of individual development in terms of job successfully held will not show evidence of voluntary acceptance of work below the level to be expected in the normal course of development. Thus, curves of the type illustrated in the accompanying diagram are most unlikely to be found in circumstances where the individual concerned expresses

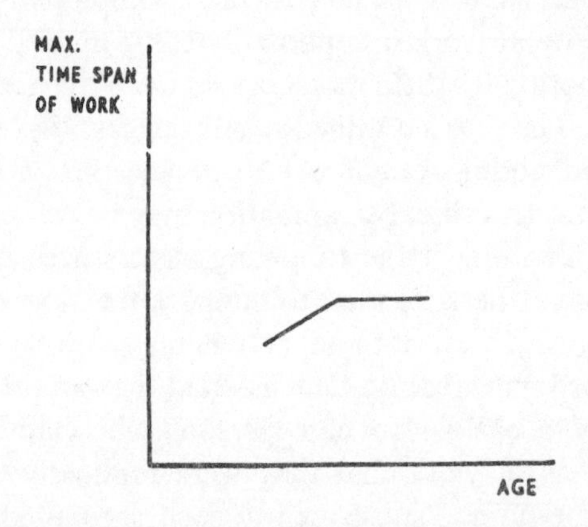

satisfaction with his work and position, and is seeking no further advancement. The anticipated outcome, according to the present line of thought, has been presented in the first example above.

The mechanisms that might make for each individual seeking his own proper level of work may, however, be considered. If a person not in training works at a level below his true capacity, he will experience strong group pressures to accept his full level of responsibility. The difficulties or problems—and sometimes even crises—that arise day in and day out in industry jeopardize everyone's economic security. As each difficulty is encountered, everyone connected with a job, managers and colleagues (and subordinates, if any), are all to some extent disturbed at their work. Everyone ordinarily wants to see the difficulty overcome as quickly as possible. The persons with the capacity to help resolve the difficulties are expected to show their mettle. And, if it is thought that some difficulties might be obviated if a given individual would only assume his full measure of responsibility, that individual will become the butt of resentment—either open or disguised.

Added to the personal effects of this resentment is the acute discomfort built up in individuals when they see crises and difficulties on the horizon that they judge they could help to prevent if they themselves had more authority. Where the capacity to do so really exists—that is to say, where it is not merely a fantasy of wishful thinking—then there is great internal pressure to take on the size of responsibility that gives the authority. Moreover, to be under-employed means the constant irritant of reviews of work at shorter periods than are emotionally acceptable. To have sufficient free play for uncertainty is a powerful driving force.

It is posited that individuals who can withstand such group and internal pressures are unlikely to be found. But it is possible that the morale of a factory could be such that a group or individuals just did not care whether or not crises and difficulties arose. In such a case it might well be that individuals could obstinately tolerate being under-employed, and indeed derive some satisfaction from it. But such situations are most unlikely to remain stable. The individuals will not remain content with their under-employment. Nor will the work get done. The usual outcome is an explosion of some kind—in the course of which either a sorting out is achieved, or there is a further build-up to another explosive outcome.

With respect to over-employment, the situation psychologically is more simple. To have too great responsibility means the anxiety-provoking situation of insufficiently frequent review of one's work, and hence the piling up of uncertainty. Even if the work proceeds satisfactorily, there still remains the feeling of being neglected or overlooked. Sufficiently frequent review of work is a necessity for the peace of mind of the individual, as much as it is a safeguard for the economic security of the organization.

IX

The foregoing analysis of the time-span capacity of individuals may suggest some reasons why changes in companies, and in the internal organization of companies, often take place in the way they do. It may be predicted, for example, that a company *that is operating successfully,* with a managing director and a team of immediate subordinates all below the age of 40 or 45, must expand and develop. If they are below 35, the company will expand rapidly. These predictions derive from the assumption that such individuals are at a stage of increasing time-span capacity, and would be seeking greater scope for their capacity. A successful company with a managing director and immediate subordinates over the age of 55 would be predicted to have strong internal forces acting in the direction of the organization remaining stable—neither contracting nor expanding—but threatened by eventual contraction if replacements are not found within five to ten years.

The implication of our assumption is clear. Whether or not changes occur in the size of business of a particular firm will depend directly upon whether the time-span capacity of the individuals in charge is consistent with the level of work being done. If their time-span capacity is growing beyond the level of work in the firm, they will grow the firm. If their time-span capacity is stable, and they are capable of doing the available work, the firm will tend to be stable. If their time-span capacity is below the level of work required, the firm will contract to a level consistent with their time-span. External considerations like market potential, while providing opportunity for growth in various directions, and setting limits in any given direction, will not cause any *particular* undertaking to expand or contract. Such a conclusion is consistent with everyday experience. Of a number of firms catering for the same market, it is frequently the case that some grow more rapidly than others, and, indeed, that some contract while others are expanding. Or, if there are numbers of firms dealing with a contracting market, it does not necessarily mean that all the firms will contract. One or more of them may well expand—either by incorporating some of the others, or by seeking other markets that they can enter with new types of product.

We may now also be able to describe in systematic terms a situation of frequent occurence in industry, and one that may be among the commonest sources of psychological stress in organization. It is likely to be a rare occurrence that the individual members who are colleagues in a firm will be of an age and a rate of time-span development so geared to each other as to allow for smooth development in which they will always remain colleagues. We may take, for example, a firm that is doing well, with a managing director of 38, working at the four-year time-span level, and subordinates of age range, say, of 32, 35, 45, and 55, doing work of the one-and-a-half-year time-span level. Such a firm will be likely to expand. Within five years, the managing director will be at the six- or seven-year time-span level. His subordinates, instead of being at one level, will have spread out. The youngest will have developed to about the four-year level, the next to the three-year level, the next to perhaps just under the two-year level, and the oldest will have remained at about the one-and-a-half-year level. The firm will have to have increased in size to hold the advancing members. The members remaining under the two-year time-span level will not be able to carry the newer responsibilities likely to be thrust upon them. The group will be faced with the difficult problem of bringing some new members over the heads of some of its older members in order to provide the economic security of a job in a successful firm for each one of them and for the members subordinate to them.

Theoretical Considerations

It is not our present task to consider means for alleviating the stresses engendered in organization by the uneven rate of development of individuals. To the extent, however, that our analysis applies, a ready technique suggests itself whereby executive groups may judge one important aspect of their own internal stability. This judgment can be made by examining the age distribution of their members in relation to the level of work being discharged. By this means, the changes may be assessed in the levels of work that the individuals will require in the approaching years—and the degree of disjunction likely to arise may be appraised. To the extent, therefore, that foreknowledge is useful, the above notions may be of some help.

CHAPTER VIII

Some Socio-Economic Implications

I

THE psychological considerations examined in the previous chapter have so far led us to the conclusion that individuals who work for their living in industry will seek work at a level that can be assessed as consistent with their current time-span capacity. Further, we have concluded that, given work consistent with his time-span capacity, a person will experience a sense of satisfaction from the fact that his work is just right for him as far as its level is concerned. The hypothesis we set out to explore goes much further, however. We have pointed to the existence of an equitable work-payment structure. Payment in accord with this structure leads, it is suggested, to an individual sense of fairness with respect to personal earnings. If we now take this hypothesis in conjunction with our analysis of the time-span capacity of individuals, the conclusion would be that each person seeks an income nicely adjusted to his time-span capacity. He will strive for that particular income which his current time-span capacity would call for within the equitable work-payment structure. If he is being paid at a level in this scale consistent with his level of work and with his time-span capacity, he will feel that he is earning a fair and reasonable income, whatever other feelings he may have about his job. It will be our task in this chapter to examine the consequences of this line of thought.

II

In our discussion thus far we have emphasized very strongly that the decisions, choices, discretion, judgment, about which we are speaking have to do with casting the die in favour of a particular course of action, and then *following that course and leaving the other possibilities behind.* This commitment to action is the kernel of the matter. In a job, decision and commitment mean expenditure of resources. It is not a matter only of thought and discussion. If inadequate or bad discretion and judgment are used, real and observable consequences follow. Work is scrapped; time is wasted; expected results are not available when wanted; orders are lost; supplies are not to hand; wrong people are selected; costly methods are used. Conversely, if good discretion is used, good results ensue. Customers are satisfied; difficulties are forestalled; progress is made; and work is experienced as running smoothly. These consequences are economically tangible. They can be checked by one's superior. And if the organization is well run, in due course they will inevitably be checked.

Good discretion contributes to the economic success of an enterprise. Bad discretion expresses itself in the concrete terms of calculable loss. Giving someone a job, therefore, means nothing less than handing over to him a part of the resources of an organization. These resources stand to be preserved or increased in value, or else diminished in value or lost, depending upon the adequacy of the authorized discretion or judgment exercised by the person employed. To the extent to which a firm calls for exercise of discretion by its members (and, as we have seen, *every* job of work calls for exercise of discretion in particular respects), it is entrusting its resources to its members, to the extent of the discretion and judgment authorized. By the same token it is relying upon those members to take care of the resources entrusted to them. Hence the premium put upon reliability. And hence also the nature of the employment contract. It is an agreement in which a person contracts to discharge his prescribed duties and to exercise due discretion in handling those resources put under his discretionary control, in return for an agreed payment.

From the foregoing interpretation of the employment contract, a very general question now claims our attention. What is the relationship between the maximum amount of the resources put within the discretionary orbit of a job, and the wage or salary that goes with that job? Common sense argues that some relationship must exist. One job carrying discretionary control over greater resources than another job must carry a greater wage or salary. But common sense is not a sufficient guide. Nor does it suggest any particular pattern of payment in relation to resources controlled. We must seek more positive leads and more conclusive evidence. At the same time, realizing that such evidence may be difficult to find, we may have to leave our analysis of this particular matter without having completed it, although we shall proceed as far as we can within the limits of our data.

Before going further, however, a point made previously must be re-stated to ensure that it is not lost sight of, since by oversight it could become a barrier to the development of our main theme. We are speaking of control of resources in terms only of *discretionary control.* A person watching over materials of great value is not *necessarily* in discretionary control over them. If he is a watchman following certain routines in guarding them, or a storeman allocating them in a prescribed manner, the discretionary control may relate solely to pace of work, and have nothing whatever to do with direct control over the valuable materials themselves. A manager, however, whose position calls for him to decide upon and implement security measures protecting the materials would indeed be exercising discretionary control with respect to them. When we speak of control of resources, it is the discretionary and not the prescribed content of a job to which we are referring.

III

What kind of connection is it to be assumed might exist between the size of the resources under discretionary control and the size of the appropriate wage—both these being expressed in terms of money? During the course of discussions on the matter, a suggestion[1] arose, which, though extremely tentative, nevertheless gave rise to certain interesting results. It was suggested that the wage might be a percentage of the possible loss involved, equal to the rate of interest at which the concern can borrow money. Even to begin an adequate exploration of such a possible connection immediately involves problems of economic theory outside the scope of the present work. Nevertheless, it was possible on the basis of data collected to make a rough empirical test of the idea, for if correct, the damage-avoidance content of hourly-rated jobs would be predictable. Working along these lines, calculations like the following were made. An hourly-rated job at, say, 4/3d. per hour, and having an eight-hour maximum time-span, would pay £1.14s. per time-span period. Taking 5 per cent as the interest on loans, this £1.14s. would represent 5 per cent of the total resources controlled within the day, or £34. It would thus be expected that the operator had discretionary control over £34 per time-span period. Or an operator earning £12.10s. per week and working a maximum time-span of, say, a fortnight, would be expected to carry discretionary control over approximately £550 per time-span period of a fortnight. Neither these figures nor others that were calculated were far removed from the actual figures that had been empirically discovered in the

[1] This line of thought was stimulated by Mr. J. M. M. Hill, the Policy Research Officer at Glacier.

analysis of damage-avoidance in the manual jobs selected for study.

Following this line of thought, the approximate resources whose protection would be called for at various time-span levels are summarized in the following table. This table assumes that the earnings are 5 per cent of the total resources controlled, where 5 per cent is taken as the rate of interest on loans.

Wage or Salary (April 1955)	*Level of Work in Time-Span*	*Earnings per Time-Span Period*	*Estimated Resources Controlled within period of Maximum Time-Span*
4/3d. p.hr.	1 day	£1.14s.	£34
5/3d. p.hr.	1 week	£11.10s.	£230
£725 p.a.	1 month	£60	£1,200
£1,150 p.a.	1 year	£1,150	£23,000
£2,300 p.a.	2 years	£4,600	£92,000
£4,500 p.a.	5 years	£22,500	£450,000
£9,000 p.a.	10 years	£90,000	£1,800,000

Some other tentative evidence for this general notion may be found if we consider three different areas of industry. Government and nationalized industries in effect borrow money at a lower rate of interest than the general run of privately-owned industries (which borrow normally at about one per cent above the bank rate). These in turn borrow more cheaply than industries with a high risk like the film industry, which may not be able to borrow money at all in the normal way, and for which special borrowing facilities may be required. And the levels of payment (taking into account all the difficulties about making such comparisons) for the same level of responsibility in the three areas is generally recognized to be different. The payment in governmental industries is lower than that in ordinary, privately owned industry, which is lower in turn than that in high-risk industries like the film industry.

Without pressing these speculations any further, one particular implication of our definition of level of work may now be emphasized. This definition in terms of discretion used, excluding as it does the prescribed result of the work, throws up a redefinition of the meaning of earnings in industry. This redefinition may be stated in the following terms. The dynamic basis of the structure of payment to those employed in industry is that of the amount of loss each one is expected to avoid by his use of discretion, rather than the amount of value he creates. (And if the above notion is correct, the wages and salaries generated are a fixed percentage of the resources put under employees' discretionary control, and that percentage is identical with the rate of interest at which the employing organization can borrow money.) This idea about earnings may run counter to classical economic theory and general belief. But it is in no way meant to imply that work is not creative. It is merely to state that although work has a creative or value-producing result, level of payment is not generated by the value of the result itself, but by the amount of loss to be avoided while producing the result.[1]

---

[1] It may be that the result of work does not enter into the question of payment because the result is always prescribed in the case of employed individuals. This prescribing of the result is one of the essential characteristics of employment. Only self-employed individuals, or Boards of Directors (on behalf of shareholders) prescribe for themselves the results they will seek in their work, and they are not paid by wage or salary. It is possibly for these reasons that special inventiveness by employed persons in producing new and valuable results—whether methods or products—going beyond the results prescribed, is rewarded by special bonuses and awards, and not by additions to wage or salary (except, of course, where promotion is given and an increase in pay results as a secondary effect of this promotion).

Moreover, it may be noted that the redefinition of work and of the responsibility that appears to be what is paid for leads to a possible basis for a national wage and salary structure. It has been suggested that such a structure not only exists unrecognized, but that it is employed intuitively in a systematic manner—trouble arising whenever there are departures from it. Once this structure is recognized and recorded, however, it can be discussed and debated in terms of the fairness or equity in the spread of money earnings as between different time-spans of responsibility.

IV

We shall now turn from these general considerations and focus our analysis in more detail upon the effects to be expected when in individual firms, or in sections of firms, payment for work departs from the equitable work-payment structure that has been described. We shall consider the effects of payment below the level expected for the level of work assigned, and of payment above this level. The analysis will continue to be based upon statements about people's feelings and impressions—a sense of fairness of payment, a judgment that work is being done effectively. Such criteria, it might be held, are not sufficient. They are too clinical, too much a matter of opinion. These shortcomings—implicit in the fact that our study is essentially a clinical one—cannot be overcome within the scope of our existing data, derived primarily from an analysis of one single firm. To minimize these shortcomings, the analysis has so far been stated wherever possible in terms of processes that may be studied in other firms. This form of statement will be continued in the analysis of the effects of over- and under-payment.

Payment in accord with the equitable work-payment scale described has been presumed to bring about satisfaction with personal earnings within the general levels obtaining, and maximum work efficiency within the particular form of organization adopted. By individual satisfaction with earnings is meant that a person considers that he is getting a fair economic return for the work he does. This is not to say that he might not be in favour of a general increase from which he and his fellow members would benefit. But, in relation to the existing general levels of payment, he will judge that he himself is getting fairly paid. And he will not feel impelled to seek an increase for himself at that time, although he might certainly support a general movement to seek a general increase for all.

Satisfaction with earnings, in this sense, would not necessarily be inconsistent with dissatisfaction in other respects; for instance, with respect to manifest recognition of status—grading, or size of office, desk, and carpet, or physical conditions of work—or with respect to various amenities and comforts, or with respect to liking or disliking colleagues or superiors. But it is suggested that if the pay is correct (in the above sense) for the work done, it will prove possible readily to resolve these other considerations. If, however, the pay is increased as well, all the issues become confused, and it will then prove difficult to resolve any of them.

An implied resolution of the problem of grievances about differentials follows from the foregoing comments about a sense of fair return for work done. The notions presented would mean that if all members were paid according to their level of work, as measured in the manner herein described, then they would all consider themselves to be fairly paid relative to each other—although, it may be repeated, this would not be inconsistent with a general desire for a general increase, which would be of benefit to all but would leave the differentials undisturbed.

Our hypothesis would also have it that to the extent to which members are appointed and paid at the level of work required, then the work of the firm will tend to be done with maximum efficiency within the limits of the form of organization adopted. By this, it is meant that managers will find that they get their work done through their subordinates with a minimum of interference from them, and a minimum of troubles, delays, and confusion. Work will be experienced as proceeding effectively. Lesser or greater payment would have a disturbing effect, and would lead to a diminution in competitiveness. These statements, which we shall examine further, are put forward only within the limits of the organizational form adopted. There are always many possible ways of organizing to get a particular task done. For example, a task can be left relatively whole, for one or a few persons to do, or it can be broken down into many simpler tasks for a larger number of people to work at. Some forms of organization may prove more efficient than others in the particular circumstances of any given firm at any given time. In the present analysis, however, these questions of organization are not dealt with, although some few comments will be made upon the subject. The point of concern is the pattern of payment that is arranged for the work allocated within whatever form of organization has been chosen.

V

Our task of analysis can be eased if we limit our considerations to persons fully established in their jobs; that is to say, to persons considered capable of discharging the responsibilities allocated to them, and not on probation or in course of training or development to learn how to do the job. By such a limitation we can more readily confine our attention for the moment to the true work content, without the added complication of special arrangements to be made for probationers or trainees. The earnings of a member in training, or appointed on probation, may be below those called for by the maximum level of work assigned, without creating any felt difficulty, because the higher levels of work given are in the nature of a test. If the member succeeds in doing them, he may then expect to be given further opportunities for work at yet higher levels, and by this means ultimately to establish himself in the position at a level of work that would in turn provide a satisfactory level of earnings. To put this in another way, a person may learn his job at a pace such that adjustments to his earnings may inevitably lag behind adjustments to the level of work he is given to do.

Turning now to members fully established in their jobs and paid below the rate for the level of work they are given to do, it would be predicted either that the members will be dissatisfied with their pay or, if they are satisfied, it will be discovered that they are performing below the level of work given them, and hence the work they do will be a source of lowered efficiency in the organization. The degree of dissatisfaction or of inefficiency will increase with the size of the discrepancy between actual earnings and the earnings called for by the work-level assigned. Much evidence for the view that dissatisfaction with pay will result has been described in the analysis of the findings from Glacier. This point need not be pursued further here. But if, as indeed may be the case, instances are found where established members remain unconcerned about differentials, although being paid below the rate for the level of work assigned, then experience suggests that the organization of the work and the satisfactoriness of the work done may leave much to be desired from the point of view of efficient operation. There is evidence to show that both the members concerned and their managers regard selection as having been ineffective. The job has been filled below the level of capacity required for the maximum level of work to be done, although perhaps satisfying requirements for the lesser aspects of the job. To the extent that the higher levels of work arise infrequently, the member may get by, he and his manager experiencing occasional crises. These crises, although not necessarily recognized in these terms, would be connected with the occasions when the higher levels of work occurred and were required to be done. To the extent, however, that the work content of a job is composed mainly of responsibilities at levels at or near the level consistent with the rate of earning, then one would expect the possibility of serious breakdown occurring in the job—either as a result of increasing difficulties arising over muddle and indecisiveness, or as a result of increasing worry and insecurity in the member in face of the demands of the job, or both.

Let us now consider the probable effects of attempts to overpay, where overpayment means payment of an individual member more than the earnings called for by the maximum level of work he is called upon to do in his job. It would be possible to get the work done satisfactorily at a lower rate of payment. And if the payment made was known by others (and payment is usually intuitively assessed), it would lead to grievances and upset arising over the vexed problem of differentials. The effect would be that of inefficiency through a combination of overpayment and a stirring up of morale problems. The problems would be resolved if the earnings of all other members were raised to an equivalent level, in which case the question of overpayment within that one organization would disappear.

The above instance leaves out of account one particular circumstance in which overpayment may not produce a disturbance. That is the situation in which a firm has a useful member whom it does not want to lose, but for whom it does not have immediately available a job consistent with the member's capacity. Temporary periods of excess payment may be tolerated under such circumstances. In conditions of full employment, however, very few individuals will accept overpayment for long, since it means they are not getting work to do that is up to their abilities and allows them to work with satisfaction or with the opportunity to advance.

A not uncommon occurrence is that one particular factory decides to pay higher wages and salaries than others in the same district, in order to attract the best of the available workers and technicians. We should expect that if, in fact, higher pay is offered for work that is in actuality held at the previous level, then the most that could be expected would be a temporary gain, and that probably an illusory one. The longer-term effects would occur in one or other of two directions. Either the other firms in the district would follow suit with equivalent payment for the same level of work, and all rates for the locality would go up. Or else, and this is perhaps the more likely effect—and the more unexpected one—the firm that had attracted the higher-level personnel would inevitably find that it was organizing its work at a higher level than was the case previously. It would be forced to do so in order to cater for the higher level of responsibility demanded by its newly attracted members. The net result of this second effect would be that the firm would then not be paying relatively higher wages and salaries than other firms—as might appear to be the case—but would rather be paying for getting higher levels of work done, though within the common wage and salary structure.

The belief would seem tenable that many instances of one firm paying apparently higher wages than the others round about are true more in appearance than in substance. The reality would more likely be (and this possibility would have at least to be considered) that what appears to be payment at higher levels is only the superficial appearance of what in reality is a different form of organization—i.e. organization in which apparently similar jobs in fact contain a higher level of work in one firm than in others.

VI

The propositions arising from the analysis may be summarized in the following manner. Differentials in payment are generated by the differentials in the amounts of resources entrusted to the discretionary control of employees. These differentials in amounts of resources are measurable in terms of differentials in the time-span of discretion. When level of work is measured in time-span of discretion, a pattern of pay differentials can be found which will be experienced as giving fair differential recognition for differences in level of work.

Two powerful forces operate to keep companies in line with this pattern of payment—economic efficiency and labour turnover. Departure from conformance to the pattern brings these forces into play: the greater the departure the more strongly are they brought into play. Payment above the pattern leads either to overpayment with consequent inefficiency if the overpayment is stabilized, or else it leads to individuals of greater capacity competing for the jobs and getting them. The presence of these individuals of higher capacity then causes the level of work to be driven upwards until conformance with the general wage and salary pattern is again established. Payment below the pattern either leads to dissatisfaction and higher labour turnover because of the awareness that other jobs carry a better return for work, or else it leads (if accepted) to a depression of the level of work achieved with accompanying recurrent crises, until conformance with the pattern is again arrived at by what is tantamount to a contraction of the organization.

These propositions, it may be noted, posit a high degree of intuitive sensitivity in people:— sensitivity about the level of work they are discharging and the rates of pay appropriate to that level; and sensitivity about the level of work that they are capable of discharging as compared with the level of work they are given to do. All of the experience in the work at the Glacier Metal Company is in line with such a view. The development of the time-span instrument provided a means for making this intuitive sensitivity explicit—it did not bring about the sensitivity. Moreover, the degree of this sensitivity may possibly be assessed with pretty fair accuracy.

Individuals ordinarily require an increase of more than 2 per cent of their pay to feel that any significant increase has occurred (for example, 1d. in 4s. an hour; or £20 increase for £1,000 per annum). And if they are asking for a merit increase, rarely, if ever, is less than a 2 per cent increase demanded. These figures suggest that discrepancies up to 2 per cent between level of work demanded and rates of pay given, or between capacity and level of work provided, may pass unnoticed, or be tolerated. Variations greater than 2 per cent will not.

We are left with the assumption, therefore, that there is about a 2 per cent margin within which static states can be achieved with respect to work level, payment, and individual capacity in industry. Changes greater than 2 per cent are perceivable, intuitively if not consciously, by the people concerned. Equilibrium is disturbed, either by demands from individuals for adjustments to their pay or level of work, or by inability of individuals to cope with new work demands. The disturbance in the equilibrium is proportional to the size of the discrepancy between work level, payment, and individual capacity. The longer the period of disequilibrium, the greater also is the disturbance. Temporary periods of disequilibrium, however, may be tolerated, particularly if they are explicitly recognized and accepted in view of whatever special circumstances might cause them.

CHAPTER IX

Conclusion

I

It may seem that we have assumed here a degree of reasonableness in human nature that is far out of line with the degree of irrationality generally looked for when matters of payment for work are being considered. This is not the case. We have outlined some conditions under which the relationship between level of work, payment, and individual capacity may be adjusted so as to be experienced as reasonable and just by the individual, and effective from the point of view of the economic security of the organization. We have further outlined some conditions under which pressures towards adjustments in level of work or pay, or in organization or appointments, will inevitably arise. We have not attempted to explore other conditions, in which for reasons of social and political stress, or of bad morale within an organization, or of personal disturbance in individuals, what might be perceived as unreasonable demands are made—whether demands upon employees by managers, or demands upon managers by their employees.

The foregoing analysis does lead us to ask, however, how frequently in industry disturbances arising over the failure to deal explicitly with intuitively sensed discrepancies between work level, payment, and individual capacity are fobbed off as due to the unreasonableness and stupidity of individuals or groups, or to their unfairness, unscrupulousness, or downright dishonesty. The whole force of our considerations leads us to conclude that this kind of distortion is always liable to arise if the level of work in the jobs being argued about is not kept in the forefront of discussion. The evidence from individual discussions at Glacier as well as from the great national crises that arise from time to time over wages and differentials points strongly to the fact that level of work is rarely, if ever, considered—or at least considered effectively—on an agreed basis.

Our work has taken us in the direction of emphasizing the basic importance of discovering and stating the range of level of work in each particular job as it is organized and set up. The range of level of work extends from the lowest level that would satisfy the minimum requirements of the job, to the highest level available to be allocated, or that it is planned to make available. From the analysis of the range of level of work, the wage or salary range applying to the job can be fixed by reference to the equitable work-payment structure, and an appropriate status for the job settled. The fixing of salary and status becomes an automatic matter if range of level of work is known: they are fixed by the level of work itself.

The statement that the fixing of wages and salaries could be done by reference to an equitable work-payment structure, offers no panacea for the resolution of wage and salary questions. What it does is to change the framework within which these questions may be discussed. It removes unnecessary points of argument from the discussions, and exposes the real and difficult points of argument more clearly. The unnecessary questions that are removed are those relating to wages and salaries for a given level of work. These are the issues that, it is suggested, are usually in the end settled according to an intuitively understood differential payment structure.

Equilibrium is eventually achieved within each organization, local or national negotiations dictating only the minimum levels. Argument and debate that do not take this structure into account serve more to confuse matters than to clarify them.

The real and difficult points of argument exposed more clearly for debate are three: What ought the relative levels of payment to be for different levels of work? What is the best form of organization of work in a firm at any particular time? And how can the capacity of any particular individual be determined and agreed so that he can be given a level of work, and hence of pay, suited to him? These three questions will be touched upon. None of them will be considered in a conclusive way.

II

What ought managing directors with ten-year time-span responsibilities to earn as compared with skilled craftsmen of a one-week level of responsibility; or the skilled craftsman as compared with the unskilled worker of a one-hour level of responsibility; office workers of a one-month level of responsibility, as compared with departmental managers carrying a one-year level? The question of the relative payment that ought to be made for different levels of work is one that has not been considered in the present study. It is a question of large social magnitude, very far outside the limits of this analysis of one single organization. The general wage and salary structure described is the outcome of the forces in society determining these relative levels. Analysis of the end result of the social process as it is reflected in a single firm does not, at this stage at least, provide a basis for a more general analysis of processes affecting economic life in general.

Our analysis does suggest, however, that complex forces are at work determining relative levels of economic return—and not all of these forces are readily identifiable for purposes of negotiation or legislation. In addition to the more familiar social and political factors that are taken into account in wage negotiations, or in fixing relative levels of taxation, our analysis gives evidence of strong forces of a psychological kind whereby individuals adjust their earnings one to the other by means of intuitively made comparisons of the levels of work they are doing. These intuitive comparisons must have a strong connection with individual spending-habits and requirements. It may be, therefore, that there is a systematic relationship between individual spending- and saving-patterns and individual time-span capacity. To pursue this possibility further would be to go beyond the limits of the data at present available.

III

The second question has to do with organization of work. What is the best form of organization of work in a particular firm at a particular time? This is an issue of vital importance in that the form of work organization determines the level of work available in the jobs in a firm; and the level of work sets the level of the wages and salaries available.

Whether or not a particular form of organization of work is the best is a matter of considerable judgment. In that it allows for judgment, it is therefore also a matter for debate. For instance, increasing standardization and routinization of work may lower the level of work available. In such circumstances, individuals occupying these jobs find themselves with their jobs disappearing from under their feet. This is one way of describing the process that is more commonly described as de-skilling of work. The effects of unrecognized de-skilling on the people concerned are very familiar. Stress and tension gradually increase as the individuals find their scope of work being reduced. The attempt is made to freeze the situation in order to prevent any further reduction. Restrictive practices creep in. Conversely, as has been described, increasing the level of work in jobs by reorganization may equally create stress and tension by making demands on individuals that they cannot readily fulfil. Because of these difficulties arising over reorganization, changes in establishment at the Glacier Metal Company have commonly been a matter of discussion and debate. It is held that discussion and debate to find out and to agree the best means of creating change is better than running into difficulties and then trying to straighten out the problems after they have been met. When changes in organization are agreed in this way, it gives advance warning to the members concerned—managers and employees alike. They can work together to achieve the changes under conditions that allow individuals to transfer or to be transferred to other jobs satisfactory to them. The trouble has been that organizational change, in the sense of changes in level of work, so often occurs without being noticed until stress and tension have been created. The Company is examining the prospect that a measuring instrument for assessing changes in level of work and for describing anticipated or planned changes will facilitate this process of getting consciously planned, debated, and agreed changes in work organization and method.

In a very important sense, however, this study has not entered into the question of the best form of organization of work. It has not taken up the question of quantity or amount of work to be done. How much work at any given level it is reasonable to expect a person to do in the time allowed is an issue that has not been touched upon, other than to exclude it as not having been found to relate to level of payment within the practices current in industry. But it is an extremely important matter from the point of view of organization. Quantity of work and level of work constitute the two fundamental factors that have to be taken into account in deciding upon work organization and establishment. The present study, concerned as it is with payment and status, has not dealt with quantity of work. For the limited purpose of assessing the effects on payment and status of the organization and establishment for work, it has been suggested that only the level of work appears to be relevant.

IV

The third remaining question is that of the level of work to be allocated to particular individuals in the light of their capacity. What level of work is warranted by a person? How is his capacity to be assessed? Our analysis has taken us to the point where the question: How much money is a person worth? has been translated into: What is the highest level of work that a person may expect to be accorded in a particular firm? This level of work determines the highest earnings to be expected by that person, in that firm, at that particular time. By thus putting the emphasis upon payment for work done rather than upon payment directly for individual capacity, the importance of individual capacity has not been cast aside. To say that a person gets paid for the level of work he carries, rather than for his skill, personality, experience, training, or other personal assets, does not diminish the importance of these assets. It merely separates two separate matters, and takes each of them more seriously by separating them. It takes seriously the notion of the rate for the job—solely in terms of payment for level of work done. And it takes seriously the matter of an individual's capacity—solely in terms of the level of the work available that he warrants.

By thus separating these two matters, procedures for wage and salary review are radically altered. Individual wages and salaries are usually reviewed in terms of an assessment of the personal worth of the individual—the assessment being based upon some non-defined and non-definable standards of payment for given levels of ability. The work done by the individual is taken into account as one of the factors to be considered in making this assessment. By this traditional procedure, two issues—personal worth and work done—are joined together with resulting confusion. A subordinate, dissatisfied with his review, may complain that he is worth more than he is getting. Comparisons with the earnings of others lead to feelings being aroused in terms of one person or another being considered as personally more valuable in an absolute sense. Little help is obtained by bringing comparisons of work done into the discussion, in the absence of agreed terms in which to compare levels of work. In the long run, discussion gets back to the question of individual worth as measured in money. This question is not only unresolvable: it is a breeding ground for suspicions about personal favouritism and victimization.

Separating the two issues of personal ability and work done still leaves a difficult argument, but an argument about one issue only, and with an objective foundation upon which to argue. A member can expect to receive payment for the maximum level of work he has been given, or that he is definitely counted on by his manager to do. Review of wages and salary is thus no longer a matter of what a manager says he thinks about a subordinate's value. It becomes instead a matter of assessing what he can objectively be shown to think, by assessing the maximum level of work, and any increases in level of work he has given to his subordinate. Wage and salary review is in this sense being conducted all the time—although it is ordinarily not recognized as such. It is carried on every time a manager gives a job to a subordinate. If the manager gives him a job with a higher level of work in it than he has given him before, then a wage or salary review has in actuality occurred, regardless of whether or not the procedures exist for recognizing this change.

This translation of wage and salary levels from terms of individual worth into terms of level of work done in the actual job does, however, leave much room for argument about whether an individual ought to be given a higher level of work. In the first place, it may be perfectly obvious to all, and agreed, that an individual is worthy of higher levels of work. But if higher levels are just not available in that firm, or in that particular section of the firm, to talk about wage or salary level, or personal worth, is fruitless. Consideration of the real work situation makes it possible for the subordinate and his manager to conclude whether it is wise to wait, or whether the subordinate ought to seek advancement elsewhere in the firm, or in some other firm.

When, however, opportunities for higher levels of work are available, managerial judgment of the most perceptive kind is called for—judgment about the capacities of individuals. The time-span analysis of level of work leaves managers and subordinates sharply face to face with each other over the issue of what jobs a manager gives his subordinates to do. This becomes the crucial point of consideration for individuals, as against the previous two matters—those of relative payment levels and of work organization—which are more general matters affecting small or large groups of people.

Whereas level of work done may be capable of objective measurement, the capacity of an individual to do work is not measurable in the same way. It must be assessed by judgment. The judgment must include a complex of factors in addition to capacity narrowly defined. It must take into account, for instance, the likelihood of a person's getting satisfaction out of the ways of the existing work group, and fitting into it. Our analysis of time-span capacity and its development may add another dimension to the assessment of individual capacity. But it is no different from any other aid to judging individuals—whether for allocating tasks, or for selection and appointment to new positions. They are all aids to facilitating judgment. They do not make the judgment. Any manager has to build his own team of subordinates in relation to the work he is given to do. And any organization has to build up its personnel in connection with the business in which it engages. Human judgment of this kind must inevitably remain as one of the prime factors whose quality determines the efficiency of work organizations, and the satisfaction of the individuals they employ.

Appendix

APPENDIX

An Example of Time-Span Analysis

I

In the course of analysis of the work under their control, some managers have pretty fundamentally revised their ideas about the level of work in the jobs that they have allocated, and, in a number of instances, they have been moved to recommend changes in the status and salary available for the jobs occupied by their subordinates. One example of such an analysis follows, an example that was reported to the Works Council in March 1955, in collaboration with the managers and their subordinates at whose request the analysis was done. The report is given in the terms in which it was presented to the Works Council, and illustrates a number of the difficulties mentioned in foregoing chapters. The analysis has to do with the work of the Regional Progress Officers—positions that were concerned with the interpretation of customer-delivery requirements and the scheduling of production in accordance with these requirements.

II

The report ran as follows:

You are having difficulty in reading my reports on status and grading. Some of this difficulty arises because I have not been able to give any examples; I have not given any examples because—although many members have authorized me to do so—it means publicly disclosing both the work done by the individual members, and the organization of this work by their managers.

Recently the situation has changed. There are now some instances in which managers and subordinates have tried out the time-span notion on organizational (including status and grading) difficulties. Some of this worked-through material can be used for reporting to you.

One such instance has to do with the work of the Regional Progress Officers. Discussions on the status and grading of their job were initiated by a group of three Regional Progress Officers. Some time later, and quite independently of the Regional Progress Officers, the two managers in line above them initiated discussions to clarify their own views about responsibilities attaching to progress work. These discussions were carried out with each group independently of the other, and separate reports, based on the analysis of their own views, were submitted to the three Regional Progress Officers on the one hand, and the two managers (the Chief Production Controller and the Chief Progress Officer) on the other. The present report is based on these two reports, and has been worked out together with the five people concerned.

May I emphasize three points about the following information:

(a) I have described only those aspects of the discussions that deal with time-span and the measurement of work;
(b) the aspects I have emphasized are those that have come up with great regularity in the now over 300 jobs I have explored with members in a similar way;
(c) the description could apply equally to jobs that are thought to be too low or too high in status, or to jobs that are experienced as either increasing or decreasing in responsibility.

Background

For some years there had been unclarity and lack of agreement about the status to be attached to progress work. The Regional Progress Officers considered that Grade III status implied too low a conception of the job they did. This conception seemed out of line with their being treated as rather more senior members on occasions, for example, when important customers were visiting the firm.

The matter had been raised on a number of occasions and had been taken forward to higher management, but it was difficult to resolve. One aspect of the difficulty was that of deciding just what were the important aspects of the job being done.

From one point of view, the job could be considered as a routine job of scheduling. From another point of view, however, there were important relationships with customer at stake. Different members, including managers at various levels, were described as holding different views about the relative importance of the various aspects. These conflicting views were also reflected within the individuals—it was easy to have uncertain views about the matter and to be swayed one way or another.

Even if it had been possible to assess how routine the job was or how much contact with customers was involved, there were still no yardsticks for assessing just how important was this work in comparison with jobs carried out by others. In order to try to overcome this difficulty, recourse was had to comparisons between individuals in different kinds of job—a kind of 'psychological' description of a job, that is, a description in terms of the kind of person required to do it.

But psychological description of jobs did not help. Opinion ranged from the view that very mature, reliable people with good judgment were required, to the view that what was wanted were people with suitable personalities capable of carrying out routine duties without much initiative. And to make things more difficult, even if opinions had tallied, there were no yardsticks available for measuring such qualities as initiative, stability, maturity, and good judgment.

Analysis

Because of the difficulty of measuring responsibilities in terms of the criteria mentioned above—customer contact; complexity or routineness of the job; or reliability, training, intelligence, imagination, etc. of the people required —an attempt was made to organize the facts in terms of the range of time-span of discretion. In order to do so, a detailed description of the actual responsibilities carried in the job was obtained.

It was striking that in a description of the job in terms of concrete and specific examples of work done, there was agreement between the views of the Regional Progress Officers and of their managers—and in this particular regard agreement had always existed.

This description comprised in outline the following responsibilities about which the Regional Progress Officers were authorized, and indeed were expected, to make decisions on their own initiative without reference upwards:

(a) breaking down orders where necessary into progressive schedules;

(b) checking on progress to ensure that proper deliveries are being made;

(c) handling customer queries as regards deliveries, making such decisions as required in smoothing over trouble, re-fixing schedules, changing priorities, etc.;

(d) taking such decisions as are necessary to satisfy the customer with regard to delivery, with no precise set of routines to operate in making these decisions;

(e) progressing work through final inspection, packing, and dispatch.

The main question, however, still remained—whether the level of work—or, to put it in other words, the degree or responsibility—could be measured. In order to do so, the longest-term responsibilities were sought. Again, considerable consistency was discovered between the independent assessment of the managers and the Regional Progress Officers.

The longest-term responsibility centred on those decisions about ordering in advance of customer schedules. Authority extended to the advance ordering of three months' anticipated requirements in the case of customers ordering according to monthly schedules. These decisions meant committing production in the light of the Regional Progress Officers' judgment of the reality of a customer's schedules and the likelihood of this customer's going ahead with his order as scheduled. Bad judgment in such decisions could have two serious effects. It could lead to wasted production, or the holding of excess stocks, if there was a failure to take sufficiently into account the likelihood that a customer might cut schedules. Or it could lead to a serious falling behind in production if an unduly cautious attitude was adopted and more bearings were suddenly required.

The time-span of these responsibilities was determined by looking at how the Regional Progress Officers' manager checked on their work. He frequently reviewed their manner of dealing with customers by spot checks of correspondence and phone conversations. The discretion with respect to schedules, however, could not readily be checked more frequently than once per month by reference to certain production load data that were got out on a monthly basis.

But even this month-to-month checking was cumbersome;

the work was much more satisfactory from the point of view of the manager when it was carried out in such a way as to be reviewed by the results achieved. Falling behind in production would be reviewed by reports from the firm's salesmen, who were constantly judging whether their customers were getting the delivery required. Over-production would be discovered in the analysis by the Accounts Department of work in progress and the level of stocks in Finished Goods Stores. The reports from the firm's salesmen led to review of the three-monthly load discretion carried by the Progress Officers. The review by the Accounts Department, on the other hand, produced monthly figures; but these could be judged only on the basis of a trend of results as shown over a period of two to three months.

Looked at negatively, it may thus be seen that the Company relies on its Regional Progress Officers to make decisions that, if badly made, would lead to production difficulties lasting at least for over one month, and at most for several months. Or, to put it another way, the Company is every day trusting its Regional Progress Officers to make decisions that initiate production; and the effectiveness of the decisions may not be known until from one to several months of production work resulting from these decisions have been completed—during which time the Regional Progress Officer continues with his use of discretion.

In the light of these considerations, this particular organization of the work of the Regional Progress Officer may be described as having a time-span range of one month to three months or more. It is emphasized that there could be other ways of organizing progress work that might carry a higher or lower time-span range, and—if the range reached below the one-month or above the one-year level—a higher or lower rank.

Some General Comments

A number of points may be noted in the above description. Questions such as how simple or routine, or how complex or difficult, was the work concerned were left aside. Equally, no attention was given to the level of skill or training of the persons judged to be required to do the job. All that was considered was the time-span of the actual responsibilities—and these were readily enough determined—a task that anyone occupying this particular Regional Progress Officer role was expected to discharge. The notion being put forward for you to consider is that time-span so calculated may give a direct measure of the level of work of staff jobs. On this principle, two things must be kept quite separate from each other—the level of work in a job, and the skill required to achieve that level of work.

(a) Level of work can be examined quite independently of the skill, experience, etc., required of the person to do the work, by considering level of work in terms of time-span;

(b) the question of skill and experience is limited to the selection of members to carry out particular jobs.

From the above point of view, status and payment are not given for a person's skill and experience, but for the work expected of him in consequence of the position he holds. This is not to devalue skill and experience. But it is to try to put a member's skill and experience in correct perspective—as the passport to obtaining a role, and a level of work within that role, which in turn carry a particular status and pay.

Finally, it should be emphasized that it is only in terms of detailed and specific consideration of actual responsibilities in particular jobs, along with the actual mechanisms that the manager concerned can use for assessing the member's decisions, that the time-span notion can be used.

Bibliography of the Glacier Project

BROWN, Wilfred

'Principles of Organisation', *Monographs on Higher Management, No. 5*, Manchester Municipal College of Technology, December 1946.

'Some Problems of a Factory', *Occasional Paper No. 2*, Institute of Personnel Management, London, 1952.

Exploration in Management, Heinemann Educational Books Limited, London; Southern Illinois University, Carbondale, Illinois, 1960; Penguin Books, Harmondsworth, Middlesex, England, 1965.

In Swedish translation—*Forskning I Företagsledning*, Strömberg, Stockholm.

In French translation—*Gestion Prospective de L'Entreprise*, Les Editions de la Baconnière, Neuchatel, Switzerland, 1964.

In German translation—*Unternehmensfuhring Als Forschungsobjekt*; Verlag W. Girardet, Essen, 1964.

'Selection and Appraisal of Management Personnel', *The Manager*, Vol. XXVIII, No. 6, 1960.

Piecework Abandoned, Heinemann Educational Books Limited, London, 1962.

'What is Work?', *Harvard Business Review*, September 1962; *Scientific Business*, August 1963.

'A Critique of some Current Ideas about Organisation', *California Management Review*, Fall (September) 1963.

'Judging the Performance of Subordinates', *Management International*, 1964, Vol. 4, No. 2.

BROWN, Wilfred and JAQUES, Elliott

Product Analysis Pricing, Heinemann Educational Books Limited, London, 1964.

'The Business School Syllabus—A Systematic Approach', *The Manager*, April 1964.

Glacier Project Papers, Heinemann Educational Books Limited, London, 1965; Basic Books, New York, 1965.

In Japanese translation—*Glacier Keikaku*, Hyoronsha, Tokyo, 1967.

'Consent or Command in Committee', *The Manager*, January 1965.

BROWN, Wilfred and RAPHAEL, Winifred

Managers, Men and Morale, MacDonald and Evans, London, 1943.

HILL, J. M. M.

'A Consideration of Labour Turnover as the Resultant of a Quasi-Stationary Process', *Human Relations*, Vol. IV, No. 3, 1951.

'The Time-Span of Discretion in Job Analysis', *Tavistock Pamphlets No. 1*, Tavistock Publications, London, 1957.

'A Note on Time-Span and Economic Theory', *Human Relations*, Vol. XI, No. 4, 1958.

JAQUES, Elliott

'Studies in the Social Development of an Industrial Community', *Human Relations*, Vol. III, No. 3, 1950.
The Changing Culture of a Factory, Tavistock Publications, London; Dryden Press, New York, 1951.
'On the Dynamics of Social Structure', *Human Relations*, Vol. VI, No. 1, 1953.
Measurement of Responsibility, Tavistock Publications, London; Harvard University Press, Cambridge, Mass., 1956.
In Japanese translation—*Sekinin no Sokutei*, Hyoronsha, Tokyo, 1967.
'Fatigue and Lowered Morale Caused by Inadequate Executive Planning', *Royal Society of Health Journal*, Vol. 78, No. 5, 1958.
'An Objective Approach to Pay Differentials', *The New Scientist*, Vol. 4, No. 85, 1958.
'Standard Earning Progression Curves: A Technique for Examining Individual Progress in Work', *Human Relations*, Vol. XI, No. 2, 1958.
'Disturbances in the Capacity to Work', *International Journal of Psycho-Analysis*, Vol. XLI, 1960.
Equitable Payment, Heinemann Educational Books Limited, London; and Southern Illinois University Press, Carbondale, Illinois, 1961. And in French translation—*Rémunération Objective*, Editions Hommes et Techniques, Neuilly-sur-Seine, 1963.
'Objective Measures for Pay Differentials', *Harvard Business Review*, Jan.-Feb. 1962.
'A System for Income Equity', *New Society*, 12th December 1963.
'Economic Justice—by Law?', *The Twentieth Century*, Spring 1964.
'National Incomes Policy: A Democratic Plan', *Pamphlet Published by K.-H. Services Ltd.*, May 1964.
Time-Span Handbook, Heinemann Educational Books Limited, London, 1964.
And in French Translation—*Manuel d'Evaluation des Fonctions*, Editions Hommes et Techniques, Paris, 1965.
'Level-of-Work Measurement and Fair Payment: A Reply to Professor Beal's Comparison of Time-Span of Discretion and Job Evaluation', *California Management Review*, Summer 1964.
'Two Contributions to a General Theory of Organisation and Management', *Scientific Business*, August 1964.
'Social-Analysis and the Glacier Project': *Human Relations*, Vol. XVII, No. 4, November 1964.
'Too Many Management Levels', *California Management Review*, 1965.

In Preparation

BROWN, Wilfred

Exploration in Management, in Dutch and Spanish translations.

INDEX